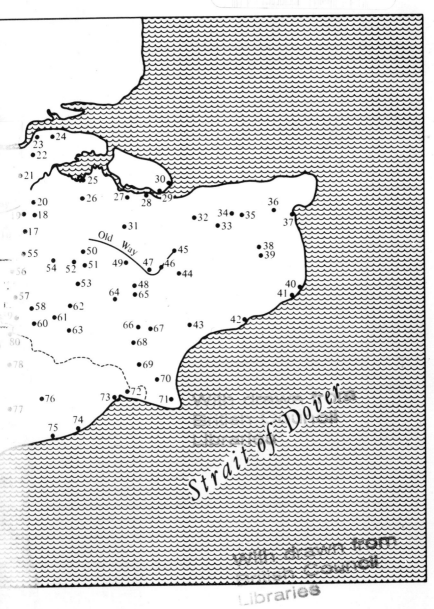

Strait of Dover

Old Way

THE
BRITISH
COUNCIL

TRUTH WILL TRIUMPH

The Countryman's Guide to the South-East

The Countryman's Guide to the South-East

John Talbot White

Routledge & Kegan Paul
London, Henley and Boston

First published in 1978
by Routledge & Kegan Paul Ltd
39 Store Street,
London WC1E 7DD,
Broadway House,
Newtown Road,
Henley-on-Thames,
Oxon RG9 1EN and
9 Park Street,
Boston, Mass. 02108, USA
Set in 10 on 12 Baskerville by
Kelly and Wright, Bradford-on-Avon, Wiltshire
and printed in Great Britain by
Lowe & Brydone Ltd
© John Talbot White 1978
No part of this book may be reproduced in
any form without permission from the
publisher, except for the quotation of brief
passages in criticism

British Library Cataloguing in Publication Data

White, John Talbot

The countryman's guide to the South-East.
1. Seasons   2. England – Climate
I. Title
574.5′43′09422   QH138   77–30547
ISBN 0–7100–8838–8

To the memory of my mother, Elizabeth,
who had green fingers

Contents

Preface

The seasonal round of the countryside, from seed-time to harvest, from summer's bounty to winter's quiescence, is an abiding source of stimulation and pleasure recorded by many observers. The rich diversity of the south-eastern counties of Kent, Surrey and Sussex, that most humanised of regions, has been the subject of many guide-books. It is seldom that the two aspects have been brought together in one book. For many years now I have had the pleasure of writing about both the countryside and the region in all its aspects and, in the course of assembling notes and observations, I have found myself quite unconsciously fashioning a personal pattern of the year, returning time and time again to specific places at particular times. Each month has become linked with places that show to greatest advantage the seasonal drama. For me, January and the Kent marshes are inseparable. February sees the herons returning to nest and the first brave show of flowers on the forest floor. March is memorable on the Sussex Downs and August on the Surrey heathlands. The deer parks are at their most majestic in October. December is made for pilgrimages along the Old Ways.

All time flows over all places and fortunate are they who find sufficient richness in the constant observation of their own parish. Such studies have been amongst the greatest in our language. Others need a change of scene, a constant exploration over new horizons. There is always so much to be learnt. I have set out for a day's delight on chalk flora and found myself completely absorbed by the behaviour of a spotted flycatcher in a churchyard. I have tramped the Pilgrims' Way looking for the winter activity of birds and returned home with my mind full of sarsen stones and the riddles of prehistory.

PREFACE

The natural world has been constantly modified by human activity, the countryside of the south-east is as much the work of man as of the natural elements that compose it. Ultimately the observer of the countryside becomes involved with the problems of conservation, whether of a footpath, an old mill or of a tract of land. The landscape is under pressure from new activities, the growth of urban areas, new roads, new forms of recreation, new modes of farming and forestry. Yesterday's hedgerow becomes today's barrier to the harvester. It is no accident that many of the places mentioned in this study are of such importance that they have gained some degree of protection as areas of outstanding natural beauty, as nature reserves, bird sanctuaries and sites of special scientific interest. Others have merited the development of nature trails and other forms of controlled public access.

Despite its location so close to the most heavily populated part of England, the countryside of the south-east is still an inexhaustible source of delight for those who seek the quiet ways, the quiet days in that most significant of pursuits, the recreation of our links with the natural world. The migration of birds, the rut of the red deer, the changing flora of down and weald and marsh, lambing time and autumn sales, fruit blossom and corn harvest, all find their setting in time and in place. Selective and personal as the book may be it penetrates to every corner of the region. I hope it will be of interest both to the armchair reader and to active explorers of the country byways.

CHAPTER 1

January

On the Norman font at Brookland church in Romney Marsh images of the twelve months of the year are beaten into durable lead. January is depicted as a two-headed figure, Janus the god, facing both ways. The countryside, also has two faces, one replete with images of the old year, seed heads, the last berries and dead leaves hanging on young oak trees. The other face looks to a new season of growing, new buds swelling on the trees, new stirring of life under the leaf litter, snowdrops emerging before the month is out.

Inland the temperatures fall to their lowest of the year, the land losing more heat than the low sun can replenish. The mean monthly reading in the High Weald at Bedgebury is just above freezing point, but when the wind turns to the east, cold air slides in from the continent bringing a reminder that only a short sea crossing divides this southernmost angle of the country from the land mass. Then the innermost valleys can record temperatures as low as $-20°C$. The earth turns to iron, the hammer ponds freeze over and even the sea water in shallow bays round the coast, such as Pegwell, may carry small floes of ice, no good for man, beast or bird. The countryside seems to hold its breath until the barometer falls again and warmer air moves up channel from the west.

Nowhere is the duality of January more apparent than in North Kent, between the Downs and the Thames estuary. A wet, cold mist drapes over the high ground, hedgerows caked with rime, each leaf bearing a crystalline halo. Dead seed heads flower anew with white frost. Icicles drip from barn roofs and freeze again into menacing knives. The woodcutter's breath hangs in the air and the sound of the saw rips through the woodland. A gunshot echoes from a copse, triggering off a flurry of birds' wings. Yet, only a few miles away to the north of the sheltered shores of the estuary, the landscape bears a kinder face. The sea holds its store of warmth longer than the land. Frosts are less severe and snow rarely lies for long. The flora is greener and fresher and there is always the chance of some of the commoner plants like ragwort, groundsel, chickweed and the dead nettles enjoying a late flowering. The bristly ox-tongue, one of the dandelion family, is usually in evidence, often flowering in the winter months. The fleshy leaves are covered with whitish pimples and bristles, an unwholesome combination but one which seems well adapted to the coastal wastes.

There are several rights-of-way following the sea walls, threading between mud-flats and marshes with just sufficient height to give vantage points for observing January's greatest bonus, the wild birds of sea and coast. As good a starting point as any is the church of St. Margaret at Lower Halstow, an old Saxon foundation with a name signifying the holy place. Its stonework incorporates Roman tiles and bricks. One of the medieval murals on the splay of an arch in the south aisle depicts a ship tossing on the waves and, above it, a dark figure looms with arms outstretched, recalling the perils of the sea. In the creeks and mud-flats beyond the church are many rotting hulks trapped in the mud, their broken ribs doing service as perching places for the inevitable gulls, but generally, in winter, this is a welcoming haven, the starting point of a two-mile walk that leads north-west towards the deserted islands of the Medway mouth.

The start is inauspicious, through a large area of wasteland in a derelict brickyard, full of wet hollows and scrub; but this is no desert for the flocks of larks, tits, finches, sparrows and wagtails darting from cover or a lapwing rising in consternation from the shelter of a broken kiln. Beyond the brickworks, reedy channels trace the boundaries of orchards sweeping down to the shoreline. The dead stalks of phragmites sway with the momentary passage of meadow pipits and sparrows and the swooping flight of reed buntings. A cirl bunting preens on a hawthorn bush exhibiting its yellow colouring before skimming down to join the flocks feeding on seeds and berries and flies.

The low-lying meadows towards the headland are sparkling with patches of standing water, favourite haunt of a flock of 200 or 300 lapwings, joined by oyster-catchers sweeping in from the sea with their staccato warning. Two dozen curlew circle sedately before joining the throng. The cries of the marshland birds all seem to have the same haunting quality, a hint of melancholy so much in tune with the sense of space and solitude that even the distant silhouette of oil refinery and power station cannot dispel. The cries get wilder still as the sea wall nears the headland. A herd of mute swans beat up the channel with vibrant wings. With the tide ebbing to reveal vast acres of shimmering mud-flats a mass of birds settle on the silky surface, all shapes and sizes from the tiny knot to the fat geese, dunlin, turnstone, redshank, shelduck, pochard, gadwall and black-backed gull. Far out on the sea's edge is a gathering of Brent geese. A small skein rises and circles several times with loud noises before splashing down on the inland pastures, causing a moment's disturbance amongst the lapwings, gulls and curlew. The Brents have deserted their Arctic homelands for these hospitable shores, rich with the eel grass which is their main food. The Medway is a major oil port and spillages in the past have contaminated the feeding grounds, but the estuary has a sufficient diversity of food to make this a wintering ground of international importance, one of the key links in a chain of European wetlands with regular counts at the January peak of more than 10,000 birds.

Each species of bird has its own favoured feeding area, the salt marsh, the brackish channels or the intertidal zone. Most numerous are the widgeon, shelduck, teal and mallard. The widgeon population can reach 7,000, feeding, like the Brent geese, on eel grass which is particularly rich in protein. They also graze on seaweeds and

3

marsh samphire. For the teal, also numbered in thousands, this is one of the main habitats, the most important in England. They feed on the seed heads of many plants but especially the marsh samphire and seablite. Their varied diet includes the mollusc, *Hydrobia ulvae*, which is also the favourite food of the shelduck, one of the most strikingly coloured of the birds, digging with strong red bill into the mud. The large population of mallard is maintained by regular releases by the wildfowlers' associations which combine their sport with a passionate interest in the general conservation of the coastal habitats and their wildlife. Much of our knowledge of the area is due to their regular observations. They are responsible, for example, for setting up a 2,000-acre reserve on the south side of the Medway for greylag geese, one of the rarer migrants, arriving from the Baltic by way of the Dutch coast. Other regular visitors include barnacle geese, goosander, goldeneye, velvet scoter, long-tailed duck and the eider. More than twenty such species are regularly recorded. One of the favourite spots for the goldeneye are the channels between the headland and the islands, ducking into the fast-flowing water for up to a minute at a time.

One of the most attractive parts of the complex Medway mouth lies to the east, sheltered from the open sea by the Isle of Sheppey, the broad channel of the Swale. The coastline here is almost devoid of housing and industry, a rarity in the south-east. In the present structure plan for the county of Kent, the Swale is planned as conservation area, making it an even more promising habitat for birds. There are several old quays and wharfs along the shoreline, such as Teynham, Oare, Graveney and Faversham, each with its quota of derelict hulks, relics of the nineteenth-century heyday of the carrying trade. The present landscape is almost entirely rural, with extensive areas of pasture and marsh. Drainage of the marshes is increasing with every year and much of the pasture is going under the plough, but, for the moment, a varied land use persists. The shoreline between Faversham Creek to the east and the Graveney Marshes to the west is signposted as the South Swale Nature Reserve with access from Graveney along the sea wall. Two miles across the estuary, on the eastern extremity of Sheppey, is another reserve at Shellness which can be reached, again by sea wall, from the isolated church at Harty. Between them lies a channel with great tidal variations, now a roaring water with yachts tacking in the fierce winds, now a calm horizon of exposed mud-flats.

4

The marshland churches are amongst the most interesting in the region, usually isolated and each with its own special character, tempting enough to delay even the most ardent naturalist from winter pursuits. Amongst Harty's treasures, for example, is a rare fourteenth-century wooden chest with a medieval joust, superbly carved on one side.

Shellness is a spit of shingle and shells curling in the shape of a comma to the south and west, away from the long-shore drift. There are literally millions of shells gathered on the ness, oyster, otter shells, cockles, mussels, sand gapers and whelks, a paradise for children but also for the birds that feed on shellfish; a haunt, too, of plovers scuttling amongst the stones.

Similar features are found on the south side of the estuary in the South Swale Reserve. About a mile west of the mouth of Faversham Creek is a succession of shelly ridges showing a sequence of plant colonisation. The outer ridges are still barren and unstable, being freshly formed by high tides and storms. The innermost and oldest ridges are almost entirely covered with creeping willow, wild carrot, sea mayweed, stonecrop, sea-beet and ragwort. Between the two extremes are ridges showing the intermediate stages of the succession. The presence of lime from the shells in an otherwise clayey area adds to the floral possibilities. On a recent January day, amongst the eight different flowers in bloom on these ridges was one head of viper's bugloss, its blues and reds brilliant against the white background.

On the seaward side, the ebbing tide leaves the mud-flats clear and dozens of dark figures are at work in the cold morning, fishermen digging for bait with fork and pail. The early birds catching the worms. Man in competition with the birds. The men use forks, disturbing large patches. The birds are more delicate, each with a bill designed to reach and open the food vital to its sustenance. The turnstone, tough and pointed, literally turns over shells and stones. The oyster-catcher, long and bright red, can reach down six or seven centimetres to its prey. The godwit beats that with ten centimetres while the curlew can reach the fat lugworms and deep-burrowing clams at a depth of fifteen centimetres. Intensive bait digging can affect bird numbers adversely and attempts have been made in some areas to control it. Birds and their feeding grounds are part of the same natural unity. You cannot conserve one without the other.

Yet it is precisely the adaptability of birds that is most heartening and maintains such a prolific wildlife in this built-up corner of England. Right in the heart of the industrial complex of refinery and cement works on the Hoo peninsula, there is a group of slurry pits at Cliffe, separated from the river only by the sea wall. In January those extraction pits are almost as exciting as the open shore. The sheltered areas of fresh water attract numbers of tufted duck, pochard and scaup, drifting on the rippling water with coot and moorhen cackling round the reedy fringes. The two latter tend to flock in winter and frequently congregate on the estuarine marshes, the moorhen feeding on land quite as much as in the water. On the artificial islands in the middle of the pits gulls gather and a line of cormorants hold their wings out like black sails. The most surprising inhabitants, however, are the flamingos, about seven of them, which have been seen for at least five years and have remained for the breeding season.

Flamingos have been reported in several places such as the Cuckmere river on the Sussex coast and at Sandwich Bay where an attempt is being made to preserve their breeding area. The all-pink plumage of the large male suggests that they are escapees from private collections, perhaps from one of the London parks. Whatever their origin, they bring a nice touch of the warm south to the darker, colder shores of the estuary. Standing on stilt-like legs, they feed by thrusting their long necks into the water and turning their large bills upside down, scooping through the water. They are exotic enough to take attention away from the herons which are always in the vicinity, either standing silently, heads hunched down, in a quiet corner of the pits, or floating gently on the air currents with long legs held back like rudders, honking as they pass.

Comparable with the North Kent marshes in size and attraction is the indented shoreline at the other extremity of the region in West Sussex, between the Selsey peninsula and Hayling Island. On the saltings and creeks of Selsey, Thorney and the complex channel of Chichester Harbour, the usual wintering birds are joined by thousands of passerines. More than fifteen species of the common wading birds are present, though in a good year that number may double. Regular visitors include whimbrels, a variety of sandpipers, greenshanks, spotted redshanks, little stints, adding to a total population of waders in excess of 25,000.

The most numerous of the duck, as in Kent, are the shelduck and widgeon, both numbered in thousands, but teal, Brent geese, pintail, goldeneye and red-breasted merganser are usually present. One of the many attractions of the area is the nature reserve at Pagham Harbour on the east side of the Selsey peninsula with grebe, eider and scoter riding on the water out to sea, as well as the varied bird life within the shelter of the extensive harbour. The birds seem equally at home on the deserted airfield that covers much of Thorney Island where curlew, lapwing and herons stalk around almost tamely, in complete charge of the runways. Even the little egret, another resident of Southern Europe, has been seen in the reedbeds of the deep that divides the island from the mainland. But the island rightfully belongs to the peewit; its image is the centre-piece of the RAF commemorative window in the Norman church by the shore of Thorney. A public footpath follows the entire shore-line of Thorney, all eight miles of it, and another follows the shore of Selsey from the village of West Itchenor round to the sand dunes of East Head, a National Trust Reserve, and West Wittering.

The activities of wintering birds are not confined to the coasts. Many of the inland water surfaces, lakes, reservoirs, hammer ponds have become havens. There are several flooded extraction pits along the Medway upstream from the estuary. The Leybourne lakes to the west of the river are the centre features for conversion to a country park, but the deep sand pit across the river near the gatehouse of Aylesford Priory is a foretaste of things to come. The company extracting sand is landscaping the pit as it works across it, and that one small pit can be crowded with mute swans, mallard, Canada geese, tufted ducks and pochards, herring gulls, black-backed gulls, black-headed gulls, coot, moorhen, cormorant and heron. The noise in a confined space in memorable, the loudest being the black-headed gulls, constantly bickering.

Follow the Medway far inland towards its headwaters beyond Tonbridge and there, just to the north of Penshurst, one of its small tributary streams leading down from Ide Hill has been dammed to form the Bough Beech reservoir, more than a mile long. It has become such a haunt of birds that although part of it is used for boating and angling, much of the east side, adjacent to the road, has been designated as a nature reserve. A pearly-grey January morning can attract as many bird-watchers as birds, lined up along the road, the name of each bird sighted being passed along the phalanx of binoculars like a password. Mallard, widgeon, gadwall, pochard, tufted duck, all familiar from our marshland jaunts. Then Bewick swans arrive with cygnets. There is a nervous search in the identification books while the experts confidently continue announcing smew, goldeneye, snipe and a red-throated diver. Two rare snow geese splash down to join the Canada geese. A cormorant perches on the marker buoy in the distance. And all the time seven heron have been standing solemnly behind us in the small upper lake, gazing at the throng. The sightings at Bough Beech include the osprey amongst other rarities. January mornings are frequently misty on these heavy, water-retentive clay lowlands, giving the setting much of its special visual quality with a backcloth of the forested ridge to the north.

The man-made lakes at Sevenoaks have none of that visual appeal, but they are even more rewarding, if that is possible, for the ornithologist. In the Vale of Holmesdale, just north of the town, the enthusiasm of Dr Harrison, and the enlightened interest of a local industrial concern, has turned a disused pit into one of the most successful bird reserves in the country. Half the nesting wildfowl in the whole region have been recorded in this one limited site and the visiting birds have included such exotica as the avocet and the Dalmatian pelican. The number of birds has increased constantly since the foundation of the reserve in 1956, as the result of careful management and a deep understanding of the birds. The natural outlines of the pits were changed to increase the number of inlets, bays and small headlands, giving shelter and privacy. Artificial islands were created with the aid of rafts.

The contents of birds' stomachs were analysed and their feeding habits identified so that appropriate plants could be introduced to the reserve. An essential basis is traditional deciduous cover such as oak, willow and alder. Then there is a need for burreed, reed-grass, sedges, bulrush, water dock, amphibious bistort, mare's tail, pond-weed and other aquatic plants typical of the older established areas like Stodmarsh on the river Stour and Amberley Wild Brooks in Sussex. Add molluscs, crustacea, insect larvae, leeches and fresh-water shrimps and a promising new habitat evolves. Though a public right-of-way cuts through the Sevenoaks reserve from the A25 road by the railway bridge at Riverhead, the full pleasure of the reserve can only be enjoyed by entry permit, giving access to the water surfaces hidden from view. The site is still shared with an angling club.

The effects of the reserve are felt far beyond its immediate confines, with increasing numbers of wintering birds on the flooded pits at Chipstead, west of Sevenoaks, and in private parkland lakes such as Chevening. No doubt, the new reservoir nearing completion at Bewl Bridge, south of Lamberhurst, will become another bird haven. This will depend partly on the control of pesticides and herbicides used in adjacent farmland. That was another part of the Sevenoaks success story, gaining the co-operation of local farmers. Another notable collection of extraction pits surrounds Chichester, in West Sussex, and this area too, being so close to the Selsey shore-line, has an abundant bird life.

The largest man-made water surfaces in the region are in Surrey, the reservoirs developed along the Thames as feeders for the canal system and then for London's water supply. They attract roosts of more than a quarter of a million gulls. Fed by the organically rich waters of the Thames, the reservoirs have developed surface algae and floating plants, an abundant aquatic fauna including the zebra mussel, first noted in Surrey Docks in 1824 and now widespread in areas up and down the Thames. This mussel is one of the favourite foods of the tufted duck which is numerous, together with the pochard, widgeon, mallard and teal. Less common are the shovelers, goldeneye, goosander and smew. The smew gathered on these reservoirs may represent more than half the total wintering in the country. Pintail is another of the species low in numbers but high in interest. The birds are best seen from the containing walls of the reservoirs and, in many cases, permits are needed from the con-trolling water authority for access. Rights of way exist around the older reservoirs like Staines and the George VI, but these inland lakes miss the atmosphere of the coastal marshes. The bird cries are matched and muffled by the constant arrivals and departures from Heathrow.

The conjunction of birds and man-made water surfaces is an ancient ones. Characteristic of the vales throughout the region are the moated houses dating from the medieval period. The ducks, geese and swans are decorative but, like the fish in the waters, they were even more important as a source of winter food at a time when most of the livestock had to be slaughtered for want of winter fodder. In the last century when such problems no longer existed, owners of the statelier mansions and castles could concentrate on the pleasure of possession and some of them built up collections of exotic birds to add distinction to their moats, such as Leeds Castle in Kent. This park is amongst the oldest in the region, being one of the three deer enclosures recorded in the Domesday survey. No deer herd is maintained now and the castle, once a royal abode, has been much modified but its great hulk of stonework resting on two islands has an ancient look that belies its frequent restoration. It still seems ready to receive Edward I and Queen Eleanor who possessed it. On the broad moat surrounding the massive stonework glide black-necked swans with fierce, red faces and black swans from the east, all hissing fiercely like guardians of the gatehouse. Canada geese loaf on the sloping pastures whilst the sounds of caged parrots and cockatoos and sundry other exotic fowl break across the wintry air. A public right-of-way cuts right across the park from the village of Leeds to a lodge gate in the east, studded by many ancient oaks and chestnut trees.

There are hundreds of moated sites in the three counties, mostly on the low-lying clay vales of the Wealden interior, though the marshes have their quota, such as Cooling on the Hoo peninsula just to the east of Cliffe. There is an especially fine group of them along the upper tributaries of the Medway along the Eden and the Kent Water, stretching across the boundary of the three ancient counties. Along the Eden are Puttenden Manor and Hever Castle, with the deserted Devil's Den near Edenbridge between them. On Kent Water is Surrey Hall and a succession of smaller sites like Basing and the Moat near Cowden. As the pressure for new lands, new manors, new revenues grew after the Norman conquest, settlers moved into the inner Weald and founded new homesteads. Many of them turned the abundant water to good use, making moats round their steads, using the dug-out soil to raise the inner ground. They formed a protective barrier against intruding animals and people and formed a natural paddock for livestock. They also supplied a source of fish-farming and a ready source of water in the event of fire, a constant hazard when timber was the main building material.

Most photographed of all is Ightham Mote three miles south of the village of Ightham to the east of Sevenoaks which uses the waters of a small tributary stream from the north.

Ightham is the perfect fourteenth-century moated house, with Tudor additions. Golden fish slide through the waters while white doves and peacocks grace the grounds. Guinea fowl and ducks splash from moat to pond, adding their comedy to the sheer beauty of the place. Many such manors were rebuilt on higher, more healthy ground in later centuries and the moats neglected, but they can often be identified on the ground.

Activity on the farms is muted. For the livestock farmer there are animals to be fed. Cattle stand about in patient groups while hay is led out to stack in racks raised about the wet ground. A flock of Southdown sheep swirl around the feed bins that have just been replenished. On some of the most modern farms, they are rolling out the new round monster bales of straw to lay out like yellow carpets for the beasts. Fruit farmers in North Kent are planting new canes for raspberries and gooseberries. New grafts are spliced on to old apple stock, the pruned stumps being coated with chemicals. Dung and piles of rotting hop vines are being led out into the fields and piles of steaming shoddy heaped under the trim hop gardens. If the weather is not too severe there is still some hedging and ditching to be done and new tile drains laid under muddy pastures. There are barns and buildings to be repaired but time, too, to peruse the catalogues of new machinery and look at the omens for the year to come.

There is always compensation for the poor grass growth, even though it means costly supplementary feed, for a mild month is not necessarily welcome. January blossom fills no man's cellar. Or again,

If you see grass in January
Lock your grain in the granary.

Growth out of season can be vulnerable to frosts later in the year. Let the seasons unroll in due order, the deep frosts breaking up the tilth, cleansing the ground. There is work to be done in the woodlands, the coppices to be cut, trees felled while the sap is low.

The best walking of the month is on the wooded ridge of light, well-drained soils that run like a green spine from the Surrey heaths of Hindhead and Leith Hill eastwards across the region towards Ashford in Kent. My personal preference is for that heavily wooded stretch that runs to the north of the Bough Beech reservoir linking Ide Hill, Toy's Hill, Mariner's Hill and Crockham Hill. On each of the hills is a memorial to a lady who was one of the pioneers of countryside conservation. On Ide Hill, a seat; on Toy's Hill, a well; on Mariner's, a monumental stone; all commemorate Octavia Hill, one of the co-founders of the National Trust, who spent the last years of her life at Crockham Hill. Toy's Hill, in her own words, was 'the first beautiful site in England given as a memorial'. Her best memorial is the large number of open spaces in the area that have been given to the National Trust.

Footpaths link the four hills, making a five-mile pilgrimage from the seat at Ide Hill to her inconspicuous grave in the churchyard at Crockham Hill. Her name is carved beneath that of her sister on a tomb beneath a yew tree, though she has a more imposing memorial in the church. The route threads a circuitous way through some of the best beech woods in the region, each clearing giving panoramic views over the Weald. Just three miles to the south are the still waters of Bough Beech where the birds are making the best of winter and the herons are waiting for February and nesting time.

CHAPTER 2

February

February has a poor reputation, shortest and worst of the months. The second month of the Roman calendar, its name is derived from the Latin 'to purify'. The Roman feast of purification was held on the 15th. The landscape is purified, too. We expect hard frosts, in spite of the hours of daylight getting longer. As the day lengthens so the frost strengthens, say the farmers. The frost kills off insects, breaks up the damp clods of earth on the tilled fields, reducing them to a fine tilth. Although there is an average temperature of about 5°C throughout most of the region, a degree or so lower in the interior, some of the hardest frosts of the year are recorded, traditionally around the 12th of the month.

Yet, in common rhymes, February has another aspect – February fill dyke. February fills the ditch not because it is a wet month; it is, on balance, one of the drier months. But it lacks the warmth to evaporate the moisture in the soil. So the ground, especially on the heavy clay lowlands, retains water, making it difficult for farmers to work and walkers to plod over soggy footpaths.

> February fill dyke,
> Be it black or be it white
> But if it be white
> Its better to like.

The countryside tradition favours a white February, the dykes filled with snow, rather than a mild, wet one. 'All the months of the year curse a fair Februeer', runs another old saying. We found out why in 1975 when an exceptionally mild month was followed by snow storms as late as May, the fruit buds were nipped, the harvest poor. Then a hot, dry summer gave light crops, thin pastures and a poor growth of roots and corn.

While frosts are good for the ground and, at the right time of the year, bring advantage to the farmer, they give no such pleasure to bird life. With frozen ground, not only are grubs, worms and insect life generally scarce, but even water is hard to find. The active hunt for food moves to the woodlands, to hedgerows and copses, around farmhouses. In the shelter of woodland, grubs may still be active in the deep crevices of tree barks and there is a plentiful supply of seeds on many plants and in the catkins of willow and hazel. There may be some berries still left on the holly and the hawthorn. Now the ivy, too, may be plundered of its purple berries. The greenish flowers of the ivy have been amongst the most conspicuous features of the woodland and now they are ripe and ready. Ivy has proved very difficult to raise from seed and it is possible that it has to pass through the digestive system of birds before it can be fertile.

A typical February scene is of a large, mixed flock of finches and tits fleeting through a woodland, always on the move, darting from cover to cover, so quickly, so often in dark coverts, that they are difficult to identify. As soon as your binoculars are trained on the right spot, the dark small shapes are off again, chuckling to each other. It is easy to miss the rarer birds amongst the hordes of sparrows, starlings, chaffinches, blue tits, black caps and buntings. One of my favourite places is by open woodland and heathland such as Holtye Common, south of Cowden, on the Kent–Sussex border. The birds rise up unexpectedly from the brown bracken fronds in large chattering clouds and seem to blow away into the birches and holly. The acrobatics in plundering the catkins are as exciting as on any bird-table. Holtye is especially rich in bird life because the open heathland is close to a deep, wooded valley which was dammed up in the sixteenth century to create a large hammer pond. The road from Cowden crosses the original dam or 'bay' at the lower end of the lake. Downstream, using the water power, stood the furnace and the forge which made the iron for the guns and cannon-balls of the Tudor navies. An imperfect gun, found buried, now stands in the grounds of Crippenden Manor reached by a track one mile to the north. Running south from Holtye Common is a Roman road which has been excavated to reveal a surface of slag and cinder taken from even older iron workings 2,000 years ago. This was an industrial area until 200 years ago. Now it is one of the quietest corners of the Wealden countryside, where the loudest noise is the drumming of the woodpecker.

The upper end of the lake is silting up, colonised by rushes and reeds and alder swamp. In the middle is a swan platform. The variety of the landscape and its food supply attracts many species of bird and other fauna. The bulrush or reed-mace is prominent with its sausage-shaped spike, ready to scatter its seeds. Break one and the white fluff inside bursts out like mattress stuffing. This is usually a still and silent place, wrapped in morning mists, so that the ear becomes a sensitive as the eye. The woodpecker drums its rhythmic accompaniment to linnet and lark, greenfinch and tree sparrow until the song thrush sings out its magnificent solo from the highest branches of the still barren oaks. The singing seems effortless. The bird just opens its throat and releases the music held within. The song gains in strength as the wind rises and buffets the trees. Storm cock, a fine name – no sound is more heartening in a wild February, a signal of defiance, an assertion that winter must end. Once I was standing by the lake so enthralled by the thrush's song that I was able to watch a tree creeper at work within a few inches of my face. His long ritual spiral up the trunk was broken by several exploratory pecks into the bark with his curved beak. He preened and had a good clean up under the wings, quite unconcerned at my presence.

Stillness is the key. There is so much to be seen standing still. The other thing to do is to select one area and watch it carefully through the seasons.

I remember an icy February day in Cobham Great Wood. The wood was once part of an extensive deer park belonging to the Cobhams, a powerful medieval family commemorated by the famous brasses in the village church. A public right-of-way from the village follows the broad track that cuts across the park from west to east in the direction of Rochester. As the track rose up through the ancient woodland that once sheltered fallow deer and a heronry, I came across the huddled figure of a boy, wrapped in a heavy coat, sandwich tin open by his side, binoculars at the ready. This was his patch. He knew it in all weathers, all seasons. He kept a list of all the birds he saw, but he was no mere collector of names. He observed their feeding habits, their nesting, their every action. He knew their songs. He had been observing both the greater and the lesser spotted woodpeckers that day. He had seen the snipe flying high towards the marshes towards the north and a heron in full sail. A flock of peewits settled on the open pastures to the west. On the fallen bough where we sat, he showed me how the nuthatch had wedged the seed capsule of the hornbeam into a crack so as to prize open the tough seed. The capsules were still there, the seeds removed. The hawfinch, with its stronger beak, needed no such aid and could snap the capsules in half and toss them aside. Being an enthusiast, the boy had tried breaking the capsules with his own teeth and found the birds made a better job of it. Berries need a close look, too. Sometimes they are swallowed whole and then disgorged in a mass of skin and pulp. But some of the hawthorn berries and rose hips are carefully eaten on the twigs, the outer skin being left intact.

Thrushes and blackbirds have a preference for the edges of woodland and seem to spend much of their time eyeing each other warily and chasing in rapid forays. They cover the pastures in an endless patrol with almost military precision, ready at any moment for flight to woodland cover. The winter flocks often have a quota of migrants of the thrush family, the smaller redwing with its conspicuous reddish flanks and the large fieldfare, grey-headed and very shy. These mixed flock can be found even on the commons in South London, such as Blackheath. Some of the most rewarding areas for bird-watching are, in fact, on the urban fringe of London and the larger towns. The higher temperatures of the towns as well as the potential pickings in gardens attract wild life. Many animals have adapted to suburban haunts, especially in the winter. Foxes thread their silent way along private highways through parks, back gardens and railway lines on the occasional foray, even venturing out into the streets. The stories of foxes loping along high streets in broad daylight are as legion as the stories of squirrels appearing on window sills. I have witnessed both events in Bromley. The animals soon learn that the suburb is safer than the country. There are fewer guns about.

A flourishing of bird song and a general intensification of feeding activity are not the only signs of the birds preparing for a new mating season. In a mild February, blackbirds have nested in Cobham Wood. St Valentine's Day falls in the middle of the month. Valentine was a Christian martyr of the third century but the sending of loving cards is more probably related to the tradition that birds select their mates on that day. A more local tradition concerning the same day is of importance to the owners of Chilham Castle in Kent. In the private woods to the west of the park is the oldest recorded heronry in England and, according to the legend, if the herons do not return to their tree-top nests by 14 February, then ill will befall the owners of the castle. Amongst the medieval families which owned the Chilham estate were the Herons, who also owned extensive land in other parts of Britain, especially in Northumberland.

To watch herons returning to the nesting sites is to witness one of the clumsiest, most comic and most enthralling sights that the month can offer. In flight the heron sails effortlessly on the air currents with slow, powerful wing beats, legs pointing backwards. When standing by the water's edge, the bird is a marvel of stillness so silent that it can easily be missed in the typical February light. But the attempt of the heron to lower itself from flight to nest is achieved with a wild panic of wings, of legs hanging ungainly as stilts as it tries to drop through the outermost branches of the elms to reach the nest on the lower branches. Often a bird will make more than one attempt to land, the first unsuccessful effort being redeemed by violent flapping of the big wings to send it soaring on a second circuit before another cautious approach. Then, above the nest, the head looks down, the long legs drop like an undercarriage and the bird plummets hopefully down. Sometimes even then it finds an intruder in the nest and the wing beats are accompanied with loud protesting honks which echo across the marshes.

Making a nest is just as elaborate a business, painfully slow. The herons steal twigs from each other's nests. I watched a heron leave its nest, drop gently into another nest just beneath him, select one long twig with careful deliberation before launching into a full, rising circle to arrive back at the upper nest where he handed his cargo over to the female there. It took him a full fifteen minutes to accomplish six more plundering forays before the rightful owner of the lower nest arrived. After a confrontation of wild wings, honks and croaks, the robbed heron stood disconsolately on the pirated nest, pecking at the remaining twigs.

This is the sort of ritual that can be witnessed in the bird reserve at Northwood Hill near High Halstow on the edge of the Hoo marshes. There are more than one hundred nests there, with an average of four or five to each tree. The binoculars soon reveal the slender necks of the herons jutting above the nests like periscopes. The only movement that betrays their presence may be the vibration of the long crest feathers in the wind. Year after year the herons come back to the same nests but winter gales and Dutch elm disease have led to the felling of many of the elms. The warden of the site hopes that the herons will begin to nest on the healthier oaks further up the hill. But managing a reserve like Northwood is a delicate matter. The first record of a nesting pair of herons was at the beginning of this century, some of the birds eventually migrating from the old heronry at Cobham. In recent years, apart from the disastrous winter of 1962–3, the numbers have risen steadily to more than one hundred and eighty nesting pairs, making it one of the largest heronries in Britain. A permit is needed to visit the nesting area and the Nature Conservancy has erected a hide so that visitors can observe the herons closely.

The rest of the 130-acre National Nature Reserve is bisected by a public right-of-way that can be approached on a footpath from High Halstow church. A mixed deciduous woodland has developed on the heavy London clay hill. The scrubby elms, oaks, ash and sycamore tangled up in a wilderness of undergrowth with fallen trees, rotting stumps, damp hollows of mosses and ferns and abundant fungi give an impression of extreme age. Yet there are no trees reaching the height and grace of those in Cobham Great Wood, for example, and records suggest that most of Northwood was cultivated until the nineteenth century, the present vegetation being secondary woodland. One of the old field banks can be traced quite easily along the crest of the hill, running parallel with the public path, capped with a line of twisted pollarded oaks. There is a distinct zoning in the wood. The summit of the hill is fairly clear, with a heathland vegetation, gorse, broom, bracken and patches of heather with some flowering in February. The oak dominates the upper slopes, giving way to the elms towards the marsh. On the lower ground is a scrubland of hawthorn, elderberry and bramble honeycombed with badger setts, rabbit burrows and foxes. The bolt holes of the badgers, their paths, the fresh markings of their paws, the fragments of their blueish hairs are evident over an extensive area of the disturbed ground, whilst the rabbits prefer the old banks on the perimeter of the wood near the open farmland.

Rabbits, together with a largely vegetable diet of grasses and leaves, are part of the badgers' winter food. Though a hibernatory animal, the badger is often active in milder winter days and cubs can be born early in the month. The winter bedding may be ejected from the sett, but the major evidence is of fresh scratching, both in the soil and on trees. The elder especially, frequently in leaf before the month is out, is a favourite scratching tree and seems to survive the treatment. Badgers are locally common throughout the south-east even in such urban areas as Richmond Park. Their territory may cover as much as four or five square miles.

A varied and sheltered woodland like Northwood Hill supports other wild life. Many birds, apart from the herons, may be seen such as warblers and whitethroats, chiffchaffs and blackcaps. Nightingales and long-eared owls are other residents. One of the most distinctive February calls is the two-toned trill of the great tit. The winter scene is enlivened by roosts of more than 20,000 starlings, blackbirds, thrushes and wood pigeons. The very accessibility of the reserve is one of the problems for its conservators. Housing estates from High Halstow have spread close to its southern margin and now there is the possibility of an oil refinery on Cliffe marshes, one of the feeding grounds of the heron, where it finds eels, minnows, sticklebacks, rudd, shrimps and voles.

Herons can be seen throughout the region wherever there are water surfaces and feeding grounds. Though they are partial migrants, some are present in every month of the year. The Arun levels, the Pevensey levels, the Loose valley south of Maidstone are amongst their favourite sites. Some nest in isolation but most group together in heronries as at Kempton Park, Virginia Water and Gatton Park, all in Surrey. Other heronries exist at Eridge, Glynde and Parham in the vicinity of ancient parkland enclosures. The birds have developed a taste for goldfish and many a private fishpond has had to be covered to avoid their depredations. But they are royal birds, a source of great pleasure. I watched one stalking through a water channel on the glutinous ooze of the Medway towering above the flocks of shelduck, knots and oyster-catchers feeding on the tidal flats. The wind curled in from the estuary with a wintry edge. Then a kestrel froze for a moment on the sea wall before zooming inland. I followed its flight past a scurry of reed buntings until it roused a flock of about 200 lapwings that rose in protest and blackened the darkening sky with their massed flight. Then two lapwings broke from the cloud and displayed their full repertory of tumbles, turns, plummets and wheels with marvellous dexterity. Two mallards took up the theme and chased each other across the salt marsh. Mating was in the air.

February may be set firmly in the calendar of winter, but the activity of the birds alone would justify its other reputation as the dawn of spring. The floral world is awakening, too. A succession of mild Februaries has made this abundantly clear, even with daffodils in bloom before the end of the month. Snowdrops and crocuses are in full bloom in churchyard and garden, with the first wild violets, lesser celandine and butterbur on the road banks. There are usually another dozen or more plants flowering at Northwood or Cobham or along the Medway shore such as red dead nettle, white dead nettle, groundsel, cow parsley, chickweed, sun spurge and the lilac ivy-leaved speedwell, coltsfoot and dandelion, daisy and shepherd's purse, many of them flowers of the waste, the early bonus of the neglected corners of the countryside. Coltsfoot and butterbur have one thing in common, that they flower before they leaf. Every month has its dominant colour and it is notable how many of the earliest flowers are yellow.

The dandelion has a special link with Kent for the gatehouse of Dent-du-Lion Castle survives in a farm group just south of Birchington on the Thanet coast. *Dent-du-lion*, the teeth of the lion, is reflected both in the colour of the flower and its tooth-shaped leaves.

There is always the chance of primroses, clustering on a sheltered bank open to the winter sun. The very name suggests spring, the first flower. Yet the earlier form of the name has no relationship to rose and appeared in early herbals as 'primerole'. Even stranger, the name of the first flower used to be attached to illustrations not of the *Primula vulgaris*, but to the daisy. There are many such examples of the transference of floral names. The daisy certainly has a greater claim to be the first flower of the year, the eye of the day, as it name suggests, opening and closing with the light. Flower names are nearly as interesting as the flowers themselves. The 'drop' in snowdrop, for example, is related to the pendants or drops that were fashionable female wear. A Sussex tradition asserts that the first snowdrop flowers on the second of the month, Candlemas Day, but plants pay more attention to the weather than to the calendar. But that tradition has links with the early Christian festival held on the same day, the festival of Presentation, when the snowdrops were strewn on the altar after removing the Virgin's image. The emblem of purification, the flower was introduced to Britain from the continent.

Even the trees are beginning to bestir themselves and nowhere is this more apparent than amongst the exotica of Bedgebury Pinetum, south of Goudhurst in the Weald. From the car park built by the Forestry Commission, the path descends into a deep valley. By Marshall's Lake, at the north end of the valley, a rhododendron is in full bloom. The old moated manor house used to stand where the lake now spreads its duck-filled waters, another manor that was made rich by the proceeds of the iron industry. Up the opposite slope by the Park Lodge, a screen of hazel catkins yellow in the wintry sun can be seen and goat willow pushes out its silvery palms. The bright yellow tracery of witchhazel and the white flower of bullace stand out amongst the shrubs. There are subtler intimations along the Cypress Avenue where the exotic foliage hangs in green curtains. On the very tips of the foliage are a myriad of small buds, bright red on the Lawson's cypress, yellow on the Nootka cypress. They always remind me of ladybirds or painted fingernails. Many of the conifers show equally rich colours in their fresh buds, such as the redwood and the Ponderosa pine. Being one of the most comprehensive collections of such trees in the country, the Pinetum offers hundres of such examples, demanding many more colours on the artist's palette than green.

There are quiet days in the month which are as soft and green as moss, days when the cushions of sphagnum moss squelch on the mole hills, a day when attention is drawn to the smaller images of the landscape, such as a prostrate tree, fallen into a dank hollow in Knole Park. It gleamed with moisture. Its death was the life of a dozen parasites. Algae, mosses and lichens competed for space.

Grey usnea grew upwards like tangled hair. Great fists of razor strop, the banded fungus, stuck out from indentations of the bark, as tough as the old timber it was feeding upon. The patches of bare wood, stripped of bark, were speckled with the orange dots of nectria. Underneath the trunk were clusters of witches' butter and, on the ground beneath, a forest of crumble cups, amongst the celandine and white dead nettle. Near my feet an oak leaf trembled. I thought it was the effect of water droplets falling from the branches above. But the leaf kept on vibrating and the earth around it heaved rhythmically. Soil broke from the ground and formed a small mound. The mole was busy, in its subterranean quest for grubs and roots. I could follow its route as the sandy heaps shuddered and crumbled into lower profile. It was so silent that I felt I could hear the mole at work. Finches and tits bustled about interested in the possibility of good pickings from the fresh excavations, but the mole had had first choice.

In the silence of that day, two does mooched close by. They nuzzled each other with soft noses and licked each other's ears. Their coats were ragged and they scratched themselves with an awkward movement of the back leg. Two stags locked horns and began to spar. But they broke off and went their separate, silent ways. Playful sparring is quite usual at this time of the year both amongst fallow and Sika deer, the most common parkland species. On the occasional bursts of warmer, sunnier weather, they may form play-rings, circling an object such as a tree stump, with kicks and leaps, making a worn path, another source of the famous 'fairy rings'. Some fraying activity is common, too, brushing the horns against tree branches, but generally the deer roam in quiet groups, the does carrying the embryo foals within them. There was little female delicacy in the doe that was plundering my pack and then butted me out of my reverie in a determined demand for food, accompanied by a plaintive, mewing sound.

The deer at Knole have become only too well adjusted to the constant stream of visitors and look for easier pickings than their natural forage. The deer in other parks, such as Parham, Petworth and Buxted, all in Sussex, have retained more of their native wildness. At Parham, the keeper leaves out some of the boughs of Scots pine that have been thinned from the forest, finding that the deer, an exceptionally dark-coated variety of fallow, enjoy stripping the barks. The red deer of Richmond and Warnham look for their winter fodder in grasses, mosses, heather shoots, bilberry, fungi, bramble, ivy and even yew foliage. Such browsing affects the growth of plants, often causing a topiary pattern as effective as a gardener's shears.

CHAPTER 3

March

March fulfils the promises that February makes. It often roars in like a lion and blows away the cobwebs of winter as it did on the first day of the month in the bird sanctuary at Selsdon. An area of mixed woodland and grassland on the very edge of the built-up area south-east of Croydon, the sanctuary has been designed by the National Trust to give protection for as many species of bird as possible, to give free access to visitors with a car park and a maze of paths. A gale was lashing rain from the west and the trees were groaning in protest. The bare woodland seemed to offer as little shelter as the open pastures. Then, with dramatic suddenness, the black curtain of cloud drew back and the sun broke through with the first real warmth of the year. Just as suddenly the air was full of song, just as if every bird sheltering there had been waiting to celebrate the moment. With the chorus came an accompanying burst of activity.

On the topmost branch of an oak, a blue tit swayed merrily on its precarious perch and explored the swelling buds. A flock of chaffinches scuffled amongst a cascade of fallen hazel catkins making only the briefest of retreats when I passed. A high metallic trill betrayed a nuthatch up in a sycamore. It darted determinedly along the whole length of the bough with a succession of dry, warning clicks before dropping like a stone and, at the last moment of its descent, swept to the base of the next tree and started another long exploration upwards.

Where the woodland gave way to an open glade, blackbirds and thrushes patrolled their territories, seeming to spend more time chasing each other about than feeding. The blackbirds were in a constant state of dark awareness, with brief, rapid flights to cover, sounding harsh warnings to the thrushes standing upright and still. With each violent gust of wind, the flock blew like leaves along the hedgerow. A busy flock of starlings, their metallic sheen gleaming in the sun, were as energetic as ever in their pastoral forays, with a few redwings still joining their winter company. Blue tit, long-tailed tit, greenfinch, tree creeper, wren, tree sparrow were all in evidence. Amongst all that song-burst was one old starling on a tree-top engaged in an extraordinary private monologue, full of pipes and whistles, chirps, chucks and quiet asides interspersed with bursts of sheer bravura cadences like a comedian holding the stage. The wind ruffling his crown feathers made him look even more like an old-time artist, only too willing to do his act.

The proximity of gardens and open farmland to this small but varied woodland encourages a variety of birds. A small, artificial pond and a number of nesting boxes are a useful addition to the habitat. Variety is the spice of life for bird activity and this is often found, as at Selsdon, remarkably close to the metropolis. There is a much trodden path, for example, at Shoreham in the Darent Valley of Kent that, in a short space of a mile, joins the banks of the river with the tree-lined ridge to the west at 150 m. It presents a microcosm of the south-east with moated farmhouses, Tudor cottages, oast houses, hops, orchards, pastures and plough lying between riverside meadows and hanger woods of beech, oak and ash, an area much loved by Samuel Palmer, the painter, who lived at Shoreham, taking his inspiration from the natural scene. His detailed sketches of the great oaks at Lullingstone and the opulent imaginings of his later watercolours, with fat sheep and golden apples, used images that can still be witnessed in this favourite weekend haunt of Londoners.

The lush gardens of the riverside cottages are rivalled by the wild display on the roadside banks of coltsfoot, common field speedwell, chickweed, cow parsley, lesser celandine and the fleshy leaves of cuckoo-pint. One garden on the right-of-way by the moated Filston Farm keeps a display board noting the first flowering of the daffodils. March is the most usual month, though an exceptionally mild winter like 1975 saw the first Lenten lilies out before the end of January.

Along the river banks is a fine display of alder and willow, happy hunting ground for wren, robin, blue tit, long-tailed tit and pied wagtail. While the tits were turning upside down in their investigation of the long, bronzed catkins of the alder, the wrens were hunting secretively in the overgrown banks, quite unperturbed by the young anglers making the most of the last days of the fishing season. Further along the river, attracted by the lake by the manor house at Lullingstone, there are moorhen and coots, tufted duck and mallard preparing for nesting sites and, in recent years, the mating display of the great crested grebe has been seen.

A particular variety of white willow tree is planted on wet riversides like these, especially where occasional flooding takes place. The cricket-bat willow is still used to make the traditional bat in local towns like Tonbridge. It is a fast-growing tree, cut down to a short trunk to produce a crop of young shoots on a seven-year cycle. The tree can achieve a girth of 152 cm in only twelve years. Amongst the recognition features of the white willow are the white hairs on the leaves.

Every bird has its favourite territory though some, like the robin and the blue tit, are conspicuous by sight and sound in every part of the one-mile walk from river to hillside. Above the beech woods and the chestnut coppices, there is a new area of Forestry Commission plantation, Meenfield Wood, Andrews Wood and Pilot Wood, introducing new conifers to the usual chalkland flora. The forest rides, open to the walker as public paths, are a haunt of rarer species. The only trouble with rare birds is that the layman like myself is always cautious of identification. We are happier with the birds we know well, but the great grey shrike is a rare winter visitor that I noted with some trepidation. More immediately recognisable were the coal tits, with their distinctive black and white heads, hurrying from cone to cone on the Corsican pines. They attacked the opening scales of the cone tips with such vigour that the air resounded with the persistent probing for seeds and mites. The blue tit activity was mostly confined to the larch where the small buds were just about to break revealing the clusters of needles, the most delicate of all greens. Amongst the robins working through the undergrowth was an immature redstart, remarkably like the robin at first glance. This rich woodland habitat may be torn apart by a south orbital motorway in the near future. Let's enjoy it while we can.

By the orchard below the woodland, the farmer is thinning out an overgrown hedgerow, not for the sake of tidiness but to remove cover from one of his deadliest enemies, the bullfinch. March in the orchards wears an unusual air of gaiety. Coloured buntings, aluminium foil, webs like candy floss, balloons carrying replicas of hawks, revolving coloured boxes all deck the trees. But they are not garlands to celebrate the return of Spring, but part of the eternal battle against the bullfinch. The flash of the finch leaving cover for a feast of new buds is as colourful a sight as any bird can offer, but the visitor's delight is the farmer's fear for the bird can strip sixty buds in a minute and seriously affect the future fruit crop. Other birds like the great tit, are suspect, too, but it is the bullfinch at the moment that falls before the gun.

March is a critical month and not just for the fruit farmer. If the winter has been wet, he hopes for drying winds. Statistically, March is one of the driest months and the soil is right for the last ploughing, for harrowing, rolling and seeding. Some farmers will take the weather and plant in February, but most, fearing late frosts, prefer to leave the sowing until March. 'Go over it once and you've got a bed', commented one, gazing at the field as smooth and brown as a board with obvious satisfaction. Then he would hope for light rains to bed the barley seed well and truly down.

The most characteristic scene of the farming round is the crop of new lambs, tottering about on long, ungainly legs before collapsing in the shelter of a wall or straw bale or a warm ewe. There is an increasing interest in breeds like the Dorset Horn which can lamb in late autumn and even give three lambings in two years. Economically it is a great advantage to lamb early. A crop of lambs in December or January is not unusual in the more sheltered areas such as

North Kent, but the lambing cycle of the traditional breeds, the Southdown and the Romney, makes March the busiest month. Down in the shelter of the coombe at Birling Gap, the sturdy flint walls, unusual in the downland scene which is remarkably devoid of such boundaries, are the focus of lambing. Straw bales are laid out in the form of a cross so that the lambs can find shelter whatever the direction of the wind. Dry, cold weather is not the danger, but damp combined with cold can be a killer. A long covered pen and an enclosure for pet lambs, orphans of the March storms, complete the picture. The scene is enacted every year, but it never fails to touch the heart. A new-born lamb staggers to its feet, tries to suckle the ewe which continues grazing, gives up and falls over within seconds.

The half million sheep that roamed the Sussex Downs have been reduced in a century to little over 100,000. Much of their traditional grassland, which has been in existence for more than 2,000 years since the earliest settlers domesticated their flocks, has been ploughed up; a war-time exigency that has become a permanency. There is more money in arable crops than in sheep. An unusual symbol of the changing pattern is a small, inconspicuous building only a mile from the farm at Birling, lying to the east up the farm track. Built of flint and brick with a long, sloping roof and a large chimney, it encloses just one room. It was a shepherd's cott, one of the last of many that once dotted the open downland. From these temporary shelters, like Scottish bothies, the shepherds tended their flocks. Now they are as redundant as the agricultural implements that are housed in Sussex museums, such as Wilmington Priory.

Quite apart from the increase of ploughed land, the decline of the sheep flocks has had another dramatic effect on the countryside. Even where the chalk grassland survives, on escarpments, on steep valley sides, the lack of grazing has allowed quick colonisers like the privet, the hawthorn and dogwood to flourish. Within a decade, they can form a thick, spiny jungle, almost impassable to walkers and riders, though they make a splendid covert for birds and wild-life generally. Beneath the scrubby layer, young saplings such as ash, oak, beech and Scots pine are seeking the light and, in time, may grow through the scrub to form a new woodland, a new leafy canopy that could eventually shade out the very shrubs that nursed them. The whole process can be studied within a few miles of the lambing pens at Birling. To the west is the chalk plateau of the

Seven Sisters where the cliff path bounces up and down over seven ridges and six valleys, two miles of walking that is made easier by the springing, close-cropped turf. Yet, three miles to the north, on the same block of hills, is Lullington Heath, a national nature reserve, which only a generation ago was covered with the same type of grassland. Now the scrubland is head high, penetrable only by the cleared rides, some of which are open to the public, a haven for tits and finches, kestrels and the yellowhammer. The heath is famous for the abundance and variety of its flora, but that is a pleasure we must return for in the summer.

It was not only the sheep that kept the Downs smooth and trim as a lawn. The rabbits did their part. The near destruction of the rabbit population, at one time greater than the number of human beings, by myxamatosis after 1954 had a similar effect. No young seedling could survive their close cropping. Each rabbit can eat a pound of green food a day. Now they are back in sufficient numbers to be regarded as a pest by farmers and gardeners. But they cannot affect the scrublands that have already been developed; they can only graze the lower flora. In March they are in the middle of their breeding season. Emerging from their burrows in hedgerow banks and disturbed ground, they venture out on to the pastures and the fields of winter wheat. There is evidence that some rabbits have adapted themselves to surface living like hares, the burrows being especially vulnerable to disease. New strains of resistance in the animals are countered by new strains of the disease. I have seen the tragic tell-tale signs from Sheppey in the north to Dungeness in the south. But still the rabbits persist. They have been a feature of the countryside since the Normans introduced them. The sale of coneys, the adult rabbit, helped many a landowner to maintain his deer parks. The word 'warren' on the map is often an indication of a medieval rabbit enclosure. Artificial pits and mounds were constructed to encourage their breeding. Even as late as the 1880s some Sussex enthusiasts tried rabbit farming as a source of a quick fortune.

The decline of the rabbit affected the many creatures that fed upon it such as stoats, foxes and birds of prey. Some species like the stoat declined in numbers, others turned to other sources of food, such as voles, rats, birds and farmyard animals. The rabbit's return has led to an increase of stoats in recent years.

The mad March days are associated with the hare as much as the rabbit, but hares are much less abundant. They can be seen, especially at dawn and dusk, in the fields north of Friston Forest, for example, but they are more likely to be seen on the marshes and levels. It is not unusual to see their paw marks forming circles in fresh March snowfall, a feature of their ritual activity in the mating season. The full beauty of a hare can only be appreciated if you have the fortune to come across one couched in its 'form', a mere hollow in the vegetation. Ears back, eyes staring, legs drawn back, the only movement is the vibration of the beating heart. As still as a Dürer etching. The stillness of uttermost tension. One false movement from the onlooker triggers those powerful hindlegs into action, launching the quarry into desperate escape. Then the run, zig-zagging across the open country, to a new haven.

There is a hummock, scarcely more than 183 cm high, on the Isle of Harty near the Thames marshes. Yet it appears on old maps as Coney Hill. One March day I was walking along the sea wall from Shellness and came across seventeen rabbits all grouped round Coney Hill, blinking at the setting sun as if in ritual obeisance. They seemed hardly aware of me and I was almost on top of the mound before the bodies stiffened, the ears pricked and the cautious hops became a frenzied scramble into the labyrinth beneath my feet. Daniel Defoe commented on these mounds or 'coterells' more than 200 years ago. They were variously attributed to burial mounds for Vikings, artificial mounds for livestock during flooding, but they are likely to be more prosaic in origin, residual masses of London clay that have survived erosion and make the perfect setting for a rabbit warren in the stiff workable clay.

The fluctuations of March weather are notorious. In like a lion, out like a lamb. Past records indicate that the month tends to be a 'lamb' at either end with a lionish spell in the middle, though its reputation for windiness is justified on the whole. It is the windiest month of the year at Kew, for example. Often in recent years the wind has turned east and given a prolonged cool spell, cold enough for snow. In Romney Marsh, home of the famous sheep breed, a shepherd assured me that if the wind was in the east 'when the sun crossed the line', it would remain there until the longest day. And when the spring equinox came, the wind was in the east and there it stayed, and with it came the blackthorn blossom. Blackthorn and the marshes go together in my mind, though the bush can be found throughout the region. It is one of the main hedging plants in marsh-land. Its importance as shelter and as a stabiliser of banks of drainage ditches was paramount and there were regulations against its removal. Its spectacular blossom is the loveliest feature of the marshland scene. The late wintry blast of March, and even later, is called the 'blackthorn winter'. Gilbert White recorded the same belief in his beloved Selborne. 'This tree usually blossoms while cold north-east winds blow; so that the harsh, rugged weather obtaining at this season is called, by the country people, blackthorn winter.' Another local name for that same weather is 'peewits' pinch' as it coincides with the peewits' nesting time, hollowing out the ground for its nest.

A more apocryphal tribute to the March wind is the old Sussex story that all the cottage windows were opened on the first day of the month to blow the fleas away. A further refinement adds that when West Sussex opened its windows, people in East Sussex closed theirs. Presumably they did it the other way round if the east wind was blowing! Appropriately, March, originally the first month of the Roman calendar, is named in honour of the god of war. The cold air masses from the east are still at war with the warmer air currents from the Atlantic, winter reluctant to give way even with the sun rising higher every day. The mean temperature is only one or two degrees warmer than February, but the longer period of light and the higher day-time temperatures have their effect on flora as well as fauna.

There is an awakening in the woods. As the three counties of the south-east have more than the national average of tree cover, there is no problem in finding a suitable patch of woodland to study. But I shall return to the Darent Valley to the old deer park of Lullingstone, making a wide detour round the golfers in the grassy glades for the high beech trees of Beechen Wood on the south perimeter of the park. There the rooks are clamouring around their high, seemingly precarious, nests, but the beechbuds remain resolutely furled. The ancient oaks, too, cannot be deceived by March sunlight. But the hornbeams are so full of buds about to burst that their canopies have an unmistakable gleam of greenness. The elderberries in the underwood have already been joined by the hawthorn, leaves opened to the light.

I return every year to one of those Surrey parishes that point like a fat finger to the heart of the Weald. Woodland was an essential part of the economy for the medieval settlements that poised on the edge of the great forest, like Limpsfield, the clearance in the elm woods. Near by was Oxted, the place in the oak woods. In the Domesday survey, Limpsfield had pasturage for 150 pigs, grunting through the acorns and beech mast. There were three hawks' nests in the woodland, too, for the delight of the manorial lord who was the Abbot of Battle Abbey in far off Sussex. The parish of Limpsfield has the elongated shape that is so typical of the Wealden villages, crossing four different geological belts, each one giving a different flora and a different use to the early inhabitants. The differences still exist: an old track ties the parish together like a thread and can be followed in search of pig pannage and hawks' nests and all the signs of the season in a variety of woodland.

The track begins on the crest of the North Downs at Botley Hill above Titsey Park in a beech wood typical of eighteenth-century plantation. Some of the trees are past their prime, but the beech, queen of the forest, is one of the most elegant of trees, frequently planted on vantage points. Stand by those gleaming trunks like columns and look south over the prospect.* The track cuts deeply into the chalk as it curls down the face of the escarpment. Part of the woodland has been felled and the seedlings from the woodland above are competing for space on the cleared ground. Beech saplings and hazel, the yew, sycamore and ash and, most heartening, young box trees full of flower, now amongst the rarer trees of the Downs, are all in evidence. Clusters of primroses and coltsfoot are enjoying an unexpected freedom. Banded fungi push out like fat plates from the rotting stumps of the felled trees and, in the damp ditches, hart's tongue fern and polypodium and male ferns are freshly green. The underside of the polypodium is packed with tiny spores waiting for dispersal. Down past the farm, the track achieves a temporary status as Pitchfont Lane until it runs into a broad shaw of oak and ash and an avenue of horse chestnuts, just breaking into leaf, part of the ring-belt of the park that used to lie to the east of the lane. Primrose and snowdrop in abundance appear along the clay vale, but now the track changes its name to Sandy Lane and starts a deep, steep climb up to the common, cutting a shadowy canyon through the sandstone. The tree roots stick out like ribs from the banks, riddled with burrows. Holly, sycamore, oak, whitebeam, ash, hazel and beech line the bank tops, hoary specimens that add to the sense of age this track gives. It needs no effort of the imagination to see the Abbot and his retainers thundering along on horseback. At

*This prospect now includes the M25 motorway.

night-time this is a highway of wildlife, in the daytime a bridlepath for the modern rider.

In the daylight, too, the early spring flowers make the most of their short growing season before the leafage turns the lane into a dark tunnel. There's cow parsley and dog's mercury, celandine and chickweed, red dead nettle and primrose, all expected and welcome. Less obvious are the small white flowers of wild strawberry and one isolated patch of shepherd's cress. My reference books say 'June to October in sandy places' for this short hairless annual with a rosette of leaves at its base. March always holds a few surprises like this and nowhere more than in these old neglected banks where the hollow ways cut across the sandstone ridges. Time, traffic and running water wore the tracks down for centuries until they were surfaced and the erosion ended. A depth of 6 m is not unusual. These man-made canyons are prominent in sandstone country and especially where the track runs north–south across the grain of the hills.

Some of the hollies at the top of Sandy Lane aspire to the full status of a tree. No shrubs these but a full 9 m or more of strong straight growth. As the track rises up to the plateau of the common, it cuts through tough, resistant bands of dark red sandstone and ironstone. The quarry face is as colourful as an oil painting. Huge hunks of ironstone stand by the roadside in the village. Nearly every house has some of the rock in its walls. The church path is composed of small slabs carefully set on end, tough, durable, attractive. The various coloured sandstones form the foundation of the timber-framed court houses that have survived from the days of the Abbot. The Old Court Lodge below the church has been identified as one of the oldest surviving houses in the south-east, possibly 800 years old, a tribute to medieval craftsmanship and to the endurance of good Wealden oak.

The dry, sandy soils of Limpsfield Common are not suited to the oak. They are better for the quick-growing birch and the Scots pine. There are some scrubby oaks there and some very good beeches and some of the rarer species like the bird cherry, but most of the tree cover is a secondary growth that has developed on the heath. Commons and charts like that of Limpsfield occur all the way along the greensand ridge as far as Hindhead. In the more open spaces, heather and bracken engage in their eternal conflict, the bracken doing specially well on the deeper soils. Bracken is a problem here, shading out the more delicate flora. Cutting it back has a beneficial effect on the rest and where there is good management heathland can be controlled to give greater amenity. Amenity in this case lies in the variety of flora and fauna that the public space can offer for the pleasure of its users. Limpsfield Common has recently come into the ownership of the National Trust, having been purchased by public subscription in 1972, only the third change of ownership since the Abbot of Battle rode this way.

Now a playground for golfer and horseman, for walker and naturalist, the common has much to offer. It is a poor day if you do not see a dozen different species of bird. The birch catkins are one of the attractions, shedding their small horned seed capsules. The long, pendant male catkin expands and opens out shedding its pollen to be carried to the shorter, scaly female catkin which will open with the tree's flowering. One of the most prolific seeders, able to cover cleared ground so quickly that it is known as the weed of the forest, the birch is also amongst the most short-lived of trees, a mere fifty or sixty years. Some of the birches on Limpsfield look much older than that, fat enough in girth to have witnessed many generations of people come and go. Older generations had other uses for the birch. Its sap was used for a mouth-wash and for wine-making. Parts of the bark were and are edible. Its young supple branches enjoyed the reputation of being able to beat out evil! A useful tree, indeed. Many of the older trees are affected by the birch bracket fungus that will drag the life out of the trees in time.

The finest woodland in the parish lies two miles to the south in the low Weald. The heavy clay soils retain moisture and minerals to sustain the growth of the broad-spreading *Quercus robur*, the pedunculate oak, the tree that supplied the timbers for the medieval houses in Limpsfield and the pannage for its medieval pigs. Staffhurst Woods has been made accessible as a public open space and the paths through it show a zoning of trees, with more beech and hornbeam, ash and sycamore on the higher ground, with an underwood of bramble, honeysuckle, hazel and elderberry. On the water channels to the south, willow and alder find their favourite habitat, but it is the oak that makes Staffhurst important. Two hundred years growing, 200 standing still and 200 year to die. That makes the birch sound as transient as a human being. All round Staffhurst the broad fields are being prepared for crops. That's what happened to the forest. For 'hurst' means a clearance in the forest. Now the clearances are greater than the forest and the remaining oak woodland is scarce.

The loveliest symbol of the month lies not in the great trees, but in one of the smallest, most delicate flowers, the wood anemone, that grows beneath them. Its very name is the Greek word for the wind. Traditionally it flowers only when the wind blows, the perfect March plant. It favours deciduous woodland. The finest display I have ever seen was in a coppice of chestnut at Otterden in Kent. By the end of March the woodman has finished cutting the whole of his 'ware' from the 'stub' leaving the standard oaks alone in the clearings. For the next few years the spring flowers like the anemone will be more prolific than usual in the coppice, having more light until the new growth rises from the chestnut stubs. Already the floor is carpeted with a promise of bluebells that another month will call into bloom.

CHAPTER 4

April

April, the loveliest name that any month bears, takes its name from the verb 'to open', the modern Italian 'aprire'. At last, despite chill east winds and late snow flurries that have beset many a recent springtime, the new warmth of the sun in the northern hemisphere is encouraging the leaf buds to open. Hawthorn and elder have already shown the way and the horse chestnut was discarding its brown protective scales long before March was out. Now all the rest of the trees in the woodlands and hedgerows follow suit, and the wych elms along the Royal Military Canal at Appledore show a startling display of red stamens, black-tipped, giving the tree a crimson glow. Clusters of oval seed develop quickly and, before the end of the month, festoon the tree with yet another eye-catching tint. The visual beauty of the elm in April makes the loss of this tree the more regrettable. Nowhere is it more noticeable than in the drained marshes of Romney and the North Kent coast where the elm was the dominant tree. Almost a half of the half million elms have been felled and many more are affected by the Dutch elm disease.

The flowering of trees is as remarkable as the more familiar ground flora. Overlooked because of their smallness in relation to the whole plant and sometimes lost visually in the bursting of leaf buds, the tree flowers are amongst April's greatest gifts. Look at the hornbeam, another characteristic tree of the region, especially prominent in the woodlands backing Romney Marsh. At first sight, the early days of the month show the buds fattening up in rich array along the twigs but gradually they open into two quite different aspects, one, the long, pendant male catkins opening with the tints of red and orange while the shorter female flowers open with the leaves and emerge with quite a different structure from the male. Tap the catkins and the pollen puffs out in yellow clouds.

The willow drapes its light greenery like a new dress reflected in the canal's surface and each day adds another unfolding until even the reluctant oak and ash join in the ceremony. Some country people look for portents of the season to come in the nesting of rooks. If they nest high, a fine summer is to come. Others prefer to watch the oak and the ash. Ash before oak, there'll be a soak. Oak before ash, only a splash. Oak and ash together, fine summer weather. The ash can be deceptive for what breaks first is its flower. Purple clusters break out from the black buds, looking as edible as a garden vegetable. Then the purple branches and a cluster of white seeds emerge while the black bud scales hang rejected. On the same tree, there may still be some of last year's winged seeds. When they eventually fall, they may remain dormant for two seasons. On two occasions at least my observation of the ash breaking has coincided with my first awareness of the cuckoo.

The ash tree is at home on chalk soils, the finest specimens occurring in the south-east, especially along the North Downs. The park woodland of Chilham and Cobham both claim trees with a height of more than 30 m. Tall and light in its canopy, the ash has a rich sub-flora. It supplies a tough and elastic wood, ideal for frames and sticks. Its leaves were used to supplement animal fodder.

Yet in spite of the beauty of the deciduous trees, their flowering and unfurling, one of the most significant trees of April is an ever-green, the yew. Early in March, the drying winds blew the white clouds of pollen across the churchyard, the smoking yew. By April the male flowers are well developed. The association of the yew with the churchyard, such a feature of the south-east, is the subject of perennial debate. A poisonous barrier to livestock, a protection for a sacred enclosure, a source of medieval bows and perks for the parson, a symbol of eternity on pre-Christian sites; each suggestion has its protagonist. The yew had its place in Easter ceremony, replacing the traditional palm of the Eastern Mediterranean, though willow 'palms' have also been used.

There are two great yew trees in the churchyard at Cudham in Kent, one of them broken by the weight of a late April snowfall in the 1950s. A local story recalls that the two trees, both with girths of about 8.2 m. formed a limbo between secular and sacred ground, the parson meeting the coffin for burial at the first yew. Nowhere is the sense of eternity felt more strongly than under the shade of the yew in Tandridge churchyard in Surrey. Seven or eight people can stand inside the immense black cavern of the hollow trunk. Its umbrage, the largest in Britain, spreads out over 26 m. and forms a canopy over the path to the church porch. According to the church notes, the rebuilding of the Saxon church had to take the yew tree into account, giving it an age of more than one thousand years, making it one of the oldest living organisms in the region. Still it sends up young shoots from the base. Still the new light needle clusters emerge from the tips of dark green foliage.

One of its rivals for the title of the greatest is at near-by Crowhurst. There are more than one hundred notable churchyard yews in the south-east, no less than four of them at Ulcombe in Kent. Ulcombe, like Tandridge, is on the greensand ridge, and though the yew is usually associated with limestone soils, it is found even on heavy clays of the Weald. It is so prevalent along the North Downs and in proximity to the Pilgrims' Way from Winchester to Canterbury that some writers have linked it with a neolithic route and used it as an indicator when other evidence of the ancient track had been lost.

The yew in all its varied forms can be seen around Doddington on the North Downs, south of Sittingbourne. A solitary giant encircled by younger trees stands at Eastling whilst in the parks of Doddington and Sharsted the immense banks of clipped yew hedge reach the level of art. The most famous yew bank, associated with John Evelyn, is in the gardens at Albury Park in Surrey, a quarter of a mile of yew trees planted for the Duke of Norfolk. The true grandeur of the yew is found on the steeper, barren, chalky slopes such as the Whites at Box Hill where it has no rival. The finest grove in Britain is in the National Nature Reserve at Kingley Vale in West Sussex. Yew woodland covers much of the upper slopes of the combe facing towards the Channel, but it reaches its climax at the bottom of the combe where the soils are deeper and moister. There the trees form a canopy so dense that no light enters. The trunks lean out in grotesque forms and their branches spread out and dip down to the ground to take root again, forming a latticed screen. Within is a cathedral gloom, a barren floor covered with the accumulation of centuries of fallen needles and flakes of bark drifting down with a soundless patter. The trees, estimated by experts to have an age of about 500 years, are descendants of the great groves that must have been a familiar sight to the earliest inhabitants of the landscape who placed their burial mounds on the rim of Bow Hill, just to the north. The contrast between that eternal darkness and the flourish of spring flowers on the open grassy swards makes Kingley Vale one of the most exciting reserves in the region. It can be reached by bridle paths from the surrounding villages of Stoughton, Chilgrove and West Stoke. The need to approach it on foot enables the vale to retain its air of secrecy and solitude.

On the banksides of country lanes, the abundance of primrose and lesser celandine is joined by tall rockcress and wood anemone, the delicate pink petals of Herb Robert and the white stars of lesser stitchwort. The stitchwort, a relation of the chickweed, actually has five petals but they are so deeply cleft that they appear as ten. Also known as the starwort, the flower was used as a remedy for the stitch. Like most of the early flowers it adapts to changes in the weather, protecting its pollen from rain by closing and drooping. The splendours of April's flora can be seen anywhere where deciduous woodland is found, but nowhere better than in a managed wood-land such as the hornbeam coppices of Ham Street, on a clay hill sloping down to the old cliff-line behind Romney Marsh. Now maintained by the Nature Conservancy to encourage its specialised insect fauna, the footpaths are dark tracks winding through an almost continuous carpet of wood anemones. By the end of the month, the coral whiteness gives way to a hazy blue of bluebells in the final flourish before the trees open into full leaf and restrict the sunlight to the ground flora.

The contrast with the dark regimented ranks of the Commission plantations at nearby Orleston Forest could not be greater. The Commission notes on Orleston comment on the ancient use of hornbeam for axles, cogs, oxen yokes and other tough usage and continues 'Nowadays there is no market for it and it is gradually being replaced by more valuable species.' More valuable, that is, in terms of quick economic returns. But look at the flowers beneath the hornbeam and then compare them with the dark void under the pines opposite and you sigh for the protection of traditional woodland practices.

Ham Street stands near the cliff-line that marks the pre-Roman coastline. South of it stretched the levels of Romney, Walland, Guldeford, once a marshland on fresh alluvial deposits until reclamation and drainage, initiated by the Romans and completed in the Middle Ages, transformed it into one of the richest pastoral areas in Britain, carrying a greater density of sheep than any other grassland. Its terminal point is the stony desert of Dungeness composed of shingle ridges built by the sea in its perpetual war with the land. The land is extending continuously, new shingle ridges being formed at the headland much to the embarrassment of the lifeboat men who have to keep replacing their shed closer to the retreating sea.

There is an air of expectancy in April in the ness. Seakale is pushing its thick purple leaves from the woody stock hidden amongst the shingle and new growth of the wood sage is showing beneath the dead stems. Gorse is in flower on the dry ridges whilst broom has evolved a remarkable prostrate form to survive the on-shore winds. In the troughs of the ridges enough moisture is gathered to make a habitat for willow scrub, sallow, reed and juncus rush. Even with modern lighthouses, nuclear power stations and a rash of fishermen's huts, the sense of space is paramount in this wildest of southern landscapes. And it will be wilder yet in the best sense of the word for Dungeness is the first landfall for migratory birds returning from the south. Tucked between the power stations and the army training grounds is a 1,000-acre sanctuary controlled by the Royal Society for the Protection of Birds. A public right-of-way runs along the northern limit of the reserve from Boulderwall Farm westwards, but permits to enter the reserve itself can be obtained on certain days from the warden at the farm, so that the visitor can follow a signed path through the shingle desert and the scrubland to a series of large pits excavated by a gravel company. Artificial lagoons and islands have been created within the drowned pits to create a habitat attractive to as many species of bird as possible. More than 270 species have been recorded on passage, about 45 of them actually nesting on the site.

The great hulk of the power stations is the backcloth to a cacaphony of wildfowl and waders. Gulls are in abundance, blackheaded with their perpetual screaming, black-backed, herring and common gulls. This is one of the rare breeding areas for the common gulls which, despite its name, is one of the less common. They are settled on their island sites, the herring gulls on the higher ground with short vegetation, the black-headed on the lower islands with denser herbage. The gulls nest early and so successfully that they are making nesting sites scarce for the long-awaited terns, the fork-tailed, shrill-voiced sea-swallows that return from their long migration in April to nest here. The larger gulls not only dominate the nesting areas, they are predatory in attacking terns' eggs. Other predators are in attendance, too, magpies, rooks, carrion crows, kestrels. The management of the sanctuary so as to give the terns the maximum encouragement to breed is one of the warden's major problems. And these are only a few of the habitues of Dungeness.

There are mallard and shelduck, oyster-catchers, pintail and tufted duck on the open pits, a rare example of fresh water on a shingle habitat. Amongst the turmoil of the black-headed gulls is one Brent goose looking incongruous. The Brents have usually gone by March but there have been regular sightings suggesting an easterly movement along the Sussex shore in Spring. Four scoters sit amongst the herring gulls. Reed buntings and meadow pipits are pottering up the shingle banks with pied wagtails flashing past. The thickets of elder, willow, hawthorn and holly are alive with yellowhammers whilst a flock of goldfinches is turning over the hay laid out for yearling lambs that have just returned from their winter pastures on inland farms. What a pleasure it would be to sit here throughout the April days and watch each new arrival! Even at the beginning of the month I saw twenty-two different species of bird including the wheatear and the chiff-chaff, true harbingers of spring. The 'big' days, to quote the warden, come later in the month with the warblers arriving, the redstarts, spotted flycatchers, firecrests, wrynecks, bluethroats and dozens of others. For many of us the 'little brown bird' is the bane of identification and bird-song written in words is not very helpful. The full enjoyment of Dungeness needs patience, time and determination, a lifetime in fact. The pleasure starts with the awareness of the sheer beauty and variety of sight and sound in this unique landscape.

The Dungeness reserve is a wonder for the botanist, too, with rare ferns and lichens and such flowers as the Nottingham catchfly to add to the more common delights of mullein, vipers' bugloss, sea campion and stinking hawks' beard, but they are most in evidence in summer.

The bird life of Dungeness affects the entire marshland area and the cliffs flanking it. An evening walk along the Royal Military Canal, especially on that four-mile stretch near Appledore now owned by the National Trust, has more than the pleasure of elms in flower, planted when the Canal was dug as a barrier to Napoleonic invasion. The conjunction of trees, shrubs, pasture and water attracts a variety of birds: tree-creeper, wren, blackcap, tit, starling, blackbird, thrush, wood pigeon, wagtail, chaffinch, bullfinch, robin, mallard, coot, moorhen, reed bunting and stonechat. Every other tree seems to serve as singing post for a robin announcing its territorial claim. The song area is its territory. One bush doesn't shelter two robins. They start nesting before the end of March and, once established, seldom move more than one mile from 'home'. The stonechat is a bird more readily associated with the summer heathlands, but it is both a summer and winter visitor, only partially migrant. Even with a red breast there is no confusing it for it has a distinctive black head.

Night falls over the canal and the bats fly overhead, diving out of their ritual circles to take a flying insect. Soon they will have competitors feeding on the wing, the first martins and swallows arriving in the middle of the month, though some have been recorded in early March. In my diary, the house martins have often arrived on Budget Day, a cheerful note on a sombre occasion. A farmer at Plaxtol near Sevenoaks has kept a record of swallows arriving and found the dominant period to be the first week in April.

Further east along the Royal Military Canal is a rare display of exotic fauna from Africa and other continents in the wildlife sanctuary of Port Lympne, an estate poised on the ancient cliff-line of the south-east before river and sea deposits cut the ancient Roman ports off from the sea. Near by the ruined walls of the Roman fort of Lemanis slump on the unstable ground towards the canal which was once an arm of the sea.

West of the mouth of the river Rother, eight miles west of Dungeness, is another notable area of shingle ridges and extraction pits which is important as a breeding area for common terns. A public footpath from Rye Harbour to Winchelsea Beach bisects the reserve. The reed beds are more extensive than at Dungeness and attract a variety of wildfowl and other birds such as warblers. There are moments here in the landscape of shingle, dune and marsh that hold memories as surprising as the beasts of Port Lympne. Only a few yards from a caravan site at Camber sands I saw two snipe take off from a particularly foul-looking ditch, more rubbish than water. On the same April day, for a bitterly cold lunch by an embankment, I sat with a shepherd who was preparing for the traditional lambing time. Never before the first of the month, he said, and prayed for a dry month. He got it, the winds remaining in the east. As we sat looking at one large ploughed field beyond the dyke, we saw heron, snipe, curlew, black-headed gull, herring gull, reed bunting, pigeon, rook, blackbird, partridge, oyster-catcher, mallard, shelduck, pied wagtail, starling. The air was full of lapwings and that most characteristic bird of the levels, the lark. And that, so to speak, was without trying, for we were deep in conversation about lambing and farming changes in the marsh. He was saying some very strong things about the men from Lincolnshire who were buying up local farms, grubbing up the trees, filling in the ponds and ditches, ploughing up the pastures and growing fields of bulbs and daffodils. They'll make it another dust-bowl, he said, an opinion no doubt exaggerated by the pride of a man whose roots lay deep in the marsh's pastoral tradition. He was especially fond of the shelduck which sat in pairs in the very middle of the freshly rolled arable, unmoved even when a hare loped across their vision. Bridleways make most of the East Guldeford level and the fringes of Walland Marsh accessible. Another footpath along the river Brede, west of Rye, leads to reedy areas where warblers abound and snipe can be heard drumming.

On either side of the marsh are cliff areas which have been protected from building. Most interesting are the glens between Hastings and Fairlight where the burns cut short, deep valleys before bouncing in waterfalls down the eroding cliffs of clay and sandstone, the oldest geological exposure in the south-east. Much of the area has been incorporated into a countryside park, including old quarries, deciduous woodland, open grassland and scrubland. But the slumping cliffs, oozing wet multi-coloured clay like toothpaste, are the main attraction. This is the kingdom of the coltsfoot, one of the few plants that really enjoys such unstable terrain, surviving its perpetual movement with a deep rootstock. By the waterfalls are ferns and liverworts, sea heath and especially horsetail, that most primeval of plants pushing its bulbous head through the cracks in the clay. On one memorable April day, I met a climber who had spent most of his sixty years exploring the cliffs with ice-axe and ropes. Whilst the quality of hand-holds, traverses and abseils may have left much to be desired, he had learnt the secrets of every wet nook and soggy cranny. He knew where to find the footprints of iguanodon, the imprint of fossilised ferns, the nesting sites of kestrel, raven and gull. His only complaint was the gorse and bramble which made his occasional careless grab for a handhold a potential hazard.

Fairlight is generally better maintained than the Warren at Folkestone, which is only too accessible to holiday-makers. The juxtaposition of chalk cliffs and wet gault clay gives a greater variety of flora than Fairlight and the jungle of scrub covering the fallen rocks is better cover for birds than pedestrians. Its flora contains the largest polypodum and hart's tongue fern I have seen. The cliff top is a fine vantage point for bird-watachers, especially as lesser black-backed gulls have nested on ledges on the cliff face and fulmars, rare in the south-east, have been reported in the same area.

Two other coastal areas compare in importance with Dungeness as migration routes. One is at Pagham Harbour in West Sussex, the other at Sandwich Bay in East Kent, on the shingle and dunes at the mouth of the river Stour. The bird reserve at Sandwich Bay has as incongruous a setting as Dungeness. To the north is a hovercraft terminal, to the south, golf courses. To the west is the industrial estate of Richborough Port and yet another power station. The nearest access point is New Downs Farm, east of Sandwich. From the farm, the path zig-zags by drainage channels for about two miles before the sign of the National Nature Reserve is reached. The scolding of warblers is apparent as soon as you cross the perimeter channel. Much of the reserve is composed of old dune ridges with a flora rich and varied enough to make it a site of special scientific interest. In the troughs of the dunes, especially, there is a summer flowering of less common flora such as marsh orchids and sharp sea rush. Part of the ness to the north is owned by the National Trust, but most of the area is managed by the Royal Society for the Protection of Birds. Dry shingle ridges festooned with sea holly and salt marsh add to the reserve's habitats. At low tide, the mud flats seem to reach right across the shallow bay to Pegwell, a popular feeding ground for migrant wildfowl. A colony of little terns nest amongst the shelly debris above the tidal limit.

Sandwich Bay is the south-easterly end of a broad belt of levels and marshes along the line of the Wantsum Channel, once an arm of the sea, with Roman forts at either end. There have been April days when it seemed the sea had reclaimed its ancient territory with the fields flooded following winter rains and late snow, a not uncommon feature of the north-east corner of Kent.

A walk along the retaining dykes, such as the Abbot's Wall and the Monks' Wall, first constructed by the monks of Minster to reclaim the land, was a journey through wildfowl and waders. Shelduck were paddling in fields of cabbages joined by a patrol of oyster-catchers zooming in from the bay. In the blackthorn bushes along the dyke, a mixed flock of small birds chattered through the sunset, yellowhammers, meadow pipits, reed buntings, joined by the exciting intrusion of yellow wagtails, birds which find their nesting sites in precisely such areas, wet levels near the coast. The whole of the channel along the Wantsum up to Reculver and along the Stour to Fordwich and Canterbury is a staging post for the April invaders.

Four hundred acres of marshland near Stodmarsh, downstream from Canterbury, have been developed as another National Nature Reserve. The lagoons and reedbeds owe their origin to mining subsidence from the colliery at Chislet and have been used as the source of an artificial wetland habitat much needed in a region where the natural wetlands have become a rarity due to the drainage of agricultural land. Apart from wintering fowl such as mallard, teal, shoveler and widgeon on the flooded meadows, pochard and tufted duck on the deeper lagoons, the site is visited by rarer species such as the garganey, the osprey, marsh and hen harriers. Rarer breeding species include bittern, snipe, bearded tit, sedge warbler and reed warbler. A variety of feeding stuff is supplied by aquatic plants including some of the more uncommon species such as bogbean, greater bladderwort, frogbit and flowering rush. The reed swamp habitat is maintained by the Nature Conservancy using a variety of techniques, regular grazing by cattle, burning and cutting of the coarser vegetation to encourage the rarer plants. The best vantage point available to the public is once more the river wall and the protective barrier known as the Lampen Wall.

Further upstream, the conjunction of nature reserve and industrial site is taken one imaginative step further where the Central Electricity Generating Board has opened up a nature trail alongside the Canterbury Power Station within a mile of the city. Forty-six acres of old gravel workings alongside the Stour have been transformed into an attraction for anglers and naturalists, yet another link in the chain of wetlands that makes this corner of Kent so rewarding.

The most southerly of the forelands is in the far west at Selsey Bill. Most of the West Sussex coast has been built over following the resort development of the nineteenth century, but between Selsey and Bognor is an area of saltmarsh and shingle bars that was once a medieval haven. It was reclaimed for farmland in 1873 but the sea wall was breached in 1910. Since then it has remained a tidal inlet known as Pagham Harbour. Seven hundred acres of it has been declared a Local Nature Reserve, ranging from low tidal flats covered daily by the sea, to higher areas only reached by the highest tides. Earth embankments, shingle bars and islands complete the picture. On the higher mud-flats are plants like the cord grass; on the lower, the green algae, a valuable food for wildfowl.

Many plants mean many birds and April in Pagham is a banquet for naturalists, with access made easy by a four-mile footpath that follows the entire perimeter of the inlet from the isolated church of Church Norton north to Pagham and its bungalows and chalets. A car park and information centre have been set up by the road to Selsey.

On a recent mid-April day I was perambulating the reserve when bird-watchers were as thick on the ground as the birds themselves. The Isabella shrike had been reported in the local press and the binoculars were trained in deadly earnest for this very rare bird. Many of the watchers were quite disconsolate when the day passed with no sighting. Yet all around us was a procession of shelduck, godwit, knot, sanderling, oyster-catcher, ringed plover, marsh bunting, firecrest and goldcrest. Out to sea, red-breasted mergansers and great crested grebes rode like ships at anchor. Enough there, I thought, to whet the most jaded appetite. They cheered up a bit when a sudden flash of white heralded the arrival of wheatears and then chiff-chaffs were seen flitting amongst the gorse.

One stout man, carrying an enormous amount of gear, asked if anyone had seen the bearded tits. He spoke of them like a personal possession. No one had seen them so he sat with his back to the rest and trained his telescope across the saltings. Look over there, he said, with a disgusted wave of the hand. I did. To my astonishment one green and yellow parakeet filled the vision. Pagham has many wonders. Its main interest is in the colony of little terns. About forty pairs nest on the protected shingle islands. That particular day the terns had not been seen so the following day across the peninsula on the sand dunes of East Head was especially memorable. Having explored the unusual dune area, now being restored by the National Trust after damage by winter gales and overuse by holiday-makers, I was lying on my back in the late evening sun when I heard the familiar high-pitched notes and saw, overhead, the little terns circling, heads watchfully turned down before plunging to the water to catch any unwary crustacean.

East Head is of special interest in that the history of its formation and changes of morphology have been recorded over two centuries. Over at Camber, restoration of the dunes is based on fences and the planting of buckthorn. Here at East Head, a complex network of fences and sand traps and the planting of marram grass and sand couch grass is being tried in an attempt to stabilise the moving dunes. West of East Head are the tidal inlets of Chichester Harbour, of Bosham and Thorney, a broad area of mud-flats that makes sunset so memorable. Common seals are not uncommon along the shore, most appropriate by a peninsula named after them, Selsey, the seal island.

April in the countryside has a clean, well-ordered appearance, the land cleared and cleaned ready for the growing season. Hedges are trimmed, arable fields rolled, pastures shorn by grazing stock waiting for the new grass that the April rains will hopefully bring. Hops are emerging from their rootstock, pushing through the shoddy and the compost. The hop-stringer is at work preparing the 'hills' as the ranks of string are called. The same trick of memory that associates martins with Budget Day makes me associate hop-stringing with the Grand National. The most enjoyable race commentary I ever heard was on a sunny April afternoon in a hop garden at Ulcombe in Kent, watching a hop-stringer showing his traditional skills. It looked so easy especially as he had a radio set strapped to his back. He raised the long bamboo pole and latched the string over a metal hook 5 m above the ground. A quick turn of the wrists made a simple knot then crossed the 1.5 m gap to teh next hook. With a long swishing sound he brought the string down to the peg on the ground. Another deft movement secured the taut mesh before moving upwards to make another hill. Rhythmically he pursued his labour, red face gleaming with sweat. Into the last furlong, said the radio. Swish, swish, went the pole. The ball of string was held in a satchel round his waist. He used forty of them in one day creating a web of about one thousand hop hills.

There are rare places such as Beltring near Tonbridge where a hop-stringer walks around on 4.3 m stilts maintaining the traditional method of getting access to the hop hills. The stilts are made from the same chestnut coppices that supply the hop poles. There has been a shrinkage in the hop acreage since the heyday of the nineteenth century when hop gardens were found as far afield as Farnham in Surrey and Rye in Sussex. Hop-growing is now concentrated in its original heartlands of East Kent, in the Stour Valley and along the Medway.

In the orchards, the trees sprout unusual additions in the form of plastic bags, a protection for the tender buds against late frost. Fires keep the air circulating. Farmers run the first sprays across the growing wheat. Spring crops are rolled and rolled again in a dry month to prevent wind blow. The hedgerow flowers blanch under the first onslaught of municipal herbicides and the elm scatters its seeds on the east wind.

CHAPTER 5

May

The south door of St Mary's at Higham on the Hoo peninsula of North Kent is a superb example of medieval carving. So are the pulpit and the rood screen, all showing the rough marks of the adze that fashioned them. The door is studded with emblems and ornamentation. Amongst the decorations are several small faces, some like angels, others most unangelic with foliage growing out of the mouths. In the church of St Warburgh in the same area is a similar representation, grinning down from one of the timber roof-supports, an old face, thick-lipped, broad-nosed, popping-eyed, but with foliage once more untwining from both sides of the mouth. The same essential figure is found in many churches in the region. He hides under one of the misericord seats of St Mary's Hospital at Chichester. He scowls with demonic face on one of the pews in St

Peter and St Paul's church at Charing. He smiles rosily with young face in the same church. Always with leaves and tendrils. He is the Green Man, Green George, Jack-in-the-Green, the spirit of May Day.

He is as ancient as the pagan gods, the symbol of the year's green renewal, incarnation in wood and stone of the vegetable kingdom. In human guise, decked out with foliage and flowers he used to lead the May Day dancing in Dorking in Surrey. He was the key figure in the Garland Day celebrations in Sussex. Together with the May Queen and the Maypole, he set the villagers reeling. The celebrations continue but in muted form and are sometimes postponed to a later Saturday in the month so as not to clash with the more recent ritual for the end of winter, the Cup Final. One of the most impressive is held on the village green at Offham in Kent. The village turns out to crown the May Queen, dressed in white, and the village children, dressed in red and white costumes, escort her with floral tributes. Those blossoms seldom include the hawthorn. In recent Springs the may has seldom opened its first white flowers by the beginning of the month. Perhaps it's a change in the weather pattern Perhaps it's the loss of eleven days in the calendar since the eighteenth century. Perhaps Shakespeare's merry England used the midland hawthorn which flowers before the common hawthorn. But Offham has other blossoms to hand. It is a cherry-ripe place set in the orchards of mid-Kent. There are wild cherries in full bloom along the woodland path to the church. The pears are laden with white flowers. There are bluebells smothering the coppice woodland to the north of the village with the last of the wood anemones and the lesser celandine flaking like old paint. Along the hedgerows yellow rattle and red campion, stitchwort and white dead nettle are reaching above the grasses. Wood spurge and milkmaid are enjoying the open spaces in a recently cleared woodland corner. Yet there are no oak branches or ash in leaf to bear in procession. Even the beech trees, so full of buds throughout April, have not fulfilled their leafy promise. But Offham is busy with sidestalls, hot buns and sausages and the climax of the day comes in a unique way, the tilting at the quintain. The black-dotted board swinging on a white pole on the green is a rare survival of the sport that has a pedigree as old as the Romans. The young riders gallop across the green, tilt their lances at the quintain and, with a good strike, are followed by a bucketful of water suspended from the swinging arm. The villagers erect a duplicate board so as to preserve the original.

The green at Offham is one of the many village greens of the Weald. It would be complete visually if only the church stood by its side but, as with many villages in the vicinity such as Addington and Meopham, the church is isolated from the village. I have never found a convincing reason for this pattern nor decided which came first, the village or the church. If only we knew more about the origin of village greens, we might find the answer. The green may mark the original clearing in the Wealden forest around which the pioneer settlement grew. A green looks so much more the focus of village life when the church stands close by as at Chiddingfold in Surrey and Wisborough Green in Sussex. The village greens of the south-east nurtured that other great festival of the early summer days, cricket.

In celebrating the opening of May with pageants, games and general festivity, the villages are only continuing the Roman festival of Flora which lasted for at least five days. The Romans named the month after Maia, mother of Mercury, goddess of growth and increase. When the people went to bring in May, they went to the woods and returned with hawthorn, larch, birch and other flora. One essential feature was the Maypole, symbolic, amongst other things, of the trees that were bearing new life. So May was the festival of youth. Death of the old Jack. Birth of the new. Perhaps that accounts for the different carvings in the churches, sometimes a young smiling face, sometimes an old, severe face. May is as variable as the faces. Temperatures may reach the heights of full summer and then plunge with a north wind and hint of frost. I've known Offham celebrate its May Day with overcoats and wellingtons. Rough winds can shake the darling blossoms all too quickly and turn them into a mock blizzard even, in one recent year, with a flurry of real snow.

The young May Queen wears a white dress, as she ought, for white is the colour of May. In one day on the Downs just to the north of Offham, of forty-six flowers in bloom by the middle of the month, no less than twenty-three were white. Stitchwort, wild strawberry, ox-eye daisy, wild flax, mouse-eared chickweed, goose-grass, white clover, Solomon's seal amongst them and, of course, cow parsley joining the hawthorn in transforming the hedges into a dazzling curtain of whiteness, an aisle for a bridal path.

The chalk scrubland dons the same cloak, with hawthorn, holly, elder, wild cherry and dogwood trying to outdo each other in splendour. The flower of the dogwood is not, at first sight, any more special than the others, but it has given rise to a fascinating legend. At one time, the story runs, the dogwood was a tall, strong tree and, as such, was used for the Crucifixion. Thereafter, in its shame, it was doomed to be small and stunted, never again strong enough to bear a hanging man. Its flower recalls the Cross, with two long petals, two short petals, each bearing a pink mark, the print of the nails. The stamen at the centre represents the crown of thorns.

Even the wild woods can hardly compare with the display of fruit blossom that crowns the garden of England. The orchards look as rich as clotted cream. The apple blossom, pink-tipped, soon opens to join the cherry and pear. Many of the cherry orchards have numbers on them and buyers will be looking at them with an eye to the future for, by the second week of the month, the crops will be auctioned.

Kent still has nearly three-quarters of all the cherry orchards in Britain, although, because of late frosts and other hazards, acreage has decreased in recent years. Nearly half the pears grown are in the same county and about a quarter of the apples. Kent's fruitfulness is due by no small measure to one Richard Harrys, Fruiterer to Henry VIII, or, to give him his full name, 'Keeper of His Majesty's Gardens, Vines and Silkworms'. In 1533, at the King's request, he brought new grafts of cherry and pear, pippins and golden renates from the Netherlands to a new garden at Teynham near the North Kent coast. The rich soil of Newgardens, still named on the map, is now covered by a housing estate and a small plaque on one of the walls pays a muted tributed to the pioneer. He deserves a better monument. Perhaps he has that in the orchards that spread out from his plantations to reach thirty parishes before the end of the century.

The North Kent plain around Teynham is one of the major fruit-growing areas in the south-east and there is no sign of the interest abating. New orchards are still being planted right down to the sea's edge, but the trees are more like bushes, easier for picking, with more fruit than foliage. New species like Golden Delicious are ousting some of the traditional kinds. Some are trained on wires in the espalier method. Another rich area lies in the Weald, signposted by one of the motoring organisations as the Blossom route, starting at the foot of Wrotham Hill and winding through the narrow lanes through Peckham and Matfield to Goudhurst. There are smaller areas of apple blossom throughout the south-east stretching from Ashburnham in East Sussex to Petworth in the west. But of the cider and perry for which Sussex was famous, even in the sixteenth century, little remains. From Sussex comes one of the traditional poems that puts a gardening truth in a neat nutshell.

When the apple blooms in March
You need not for barrels search;
When the apple blooms in May
Search for apples every day.

The poem was only too true a reflection of the 1975 season when a mild winter brought the first blossom out in March followed by a cold April and May that destroyed the cherry crop and decimated the apples. In that same year, some of the late blossom arrived on apple trees in June, together with some small apples from the earlier flowers, the only time I have seen such an unseasonal conjunction.

Fruit existed before Richard Harrys's innovations. The crab apple and the bird cherry grow wild in many a woodland copse. Fruits were introduced by the Romans and again by the Normans to be cultivated on monastic estates and in noblemen's gardens. Some of the old names, like reinette, have links with the France of the Middle Ages. Even the name of the wild cherry, the gean, has been linked by some horticulturists with the region of Guyenne, gaskins with Gascony and the May Duke with Medoc. The history of fruit is as rich as its blossom. Such names speak of the constant endeavour to find new and better fruits, not to say new fashions. Harrys was not the only seeker for new types. Leonard Mascall of Plumpton in Sussex was another introducer of apples in the sixteenth century. The agriculture college near by carries on the same tradition, similar to that of the East Malling research station in the orchards of the Medway valley.

The garden image is everywhere. The roadside verges are as varied and colourful as at any time of the year. By the end of the month, the coarser species like cow parsley and stinging nettle will dominate. But as May advances so the delicate Herb Robert, balm for all ills, offers its five pink petals and tracery leaves, joined by herb bennet, Jack-by-the-hedge, ox-eye daisy, goose grass, the big white ransoms and common sorrel. Bees and flies zoom amongst the flowers and grasses, investigating every smell and every hollow, even to dark holes in the soil.

The more open grasslands of the chalk Downs are beginning to unfold new wonders, on their thin, dry soils. I once wrote about cowslips and was taken to task by some readers for mentioning their location. The flowers are so vulnerable to indiscriminate picking by visitors. They must have been prolific once upon a time for Dorking's Jack-in-the-Green danced on cowslips. Yet there are still some places and some years, notably after a previous hot summer, when the yellow clusters are abundant enough to carpet an entire pasture. In a hidden valley-head above Otford, only a mile or so from a busy main road, the cowslips rose in thick patches rather like the cow-pats, from which they may have derived their name. They were all on the sunny slope while the opposite, darker slope was primrose territory. In one place in the valley-bottom, the two flowers grew together and there, too, was the comparatively rare false oxlip, a hybrid of the other two flowers. That same year they were just as prolific on the Sussex Downs above the Old Man of Wilmington, an even more public place. The finest display I have ever seen was on Mount Caburn, an isolated block of the chalk hills in Sussex, where it was almost impossible to avoid treading on them on the path to the Iron Age camp at the summit. The yellow carpet was touched lightly with violets and milkwort, a sight made even more memorable by the clear outlines of the ancient Celtic field system that has been in use before the Romans came.

If we need to be secretive about cowslip country, we are almost sworn to silence about our beloved wild orchids. Variable in their occurrence, both in time and place, orchids are surprisingly common throughout the region. They don't need to be sought; they announce themselves proudly, growing straight and tall above the thin grass cover. Imagine a bare hollow amongst the dunes with a sudden sight of thirty-seven heads of early purple orchid and every head a cluster of dark-stained flowers. Orchids grow on most of the southern soils, from marsh to dry heathland, but they are most abundant on the chalk. The North Downs from Kent to Surrey can show most of the fifty or more species known in Britain and Kent has two or three that are rarely known elsewhere.

The orchid is so sensitive to climate and soil conditions, needing a particular fungal growth attached to its root tubers that any interference is disastrous. Legal protection can never be enough to overcome human greed and thoughtlessness. Orchids come and go with such speed that they need constant observation to observe the season's sequence. I have often taken chosen friends to see a particularly fine display to find the flowering over, sometimes, happily, to be replaced by other species. In one field there were six different species with more than fifty flowering heads. The following year, at the same time, there were only six limp heads of the early purple orchid. One especially poor year was saved by finding, quite accidentally, no less than sixty green heads of the common twayblade under a sycamore in Sheffield Park, easily missed amongst the tall grasses in a patch between the mown paths. The common twayblade is an inconspicuous orchid with two pronounced 'blades', pollinated by flies and beetles. Hardly a collector's delight, yet that flower takes fifteen years to evolve from the seed. In the same garden, common spotted orchids stood unseen beneath one of the hundreds of rhododendron bushes on the sandy soil of the Weald.

Most of the nature reserves, where the open chalk grassland is maintained, will reward patient investigation. Queen Down Warren near Sittingbourne, Wye and Crundale Downs above Wye, Kingley Vale in West Sussex and Lullington Heath in East Sussex are such areas, the last three having nature trails or paths laid out for the public. Some orchids grow remarkably close to paths, seeming to like the compacted ground. Amongst the first to appear, even before the end of April, is the early purple orchid. Rabbits may eat the fleshy spotted leaves and birds, such as the jay and magpie, have been known to attack the stems. The man orchid seems to prefer lower slopes with deeper soils and taller grasses. It is not exciting in colour but its structure is, the lower lip forming the shape of a manikin. Many orchids take their names from the characteristic shape of the lower lip of each flower. The early spider orchid and the green-winged orchid are two more early species, the latter having similar coloration to the purple orchid, but with a much shorter stem.

The wardens of reserves wisely keep quiet about the rarer species such as lady's slipper, the lizard orchid and the military orchid. The enthusiast ought to join the local naturalist clubs to pursue such an interest.

For many country ramblers, May is bluebell time. The flower is associated with woodland and where it occurs in hedgerow banks and waste ground it is usually evidence of previous woodland cover. The open spaces of beech woodland suits it well, gathering the sunlight before the leaves cast their full shadow. The last of the bluebells is the last of spring. Summer's green rankness takes over. There are few displays to match those in old deciduous woodland such as Eastwell and the King's Forest at Challock in Kent, or Slindon and the beech woods of West Sussex. Yet the bluebell can be even more prolific in the coppiced woodland that is such a feature of the south-east, especially when the chestnut poles have been cut afresh. Then the bluebell has all the nourishment and all the light it needs to colonise all the available ground.

Cowslips and orchids may be the most delectable of downland flora, but the common blue butterfly and the clouded yellow that are floating gently over the warm evening slopes are looking for more mundane flora such as the birdsfoot trefoil with its red and yellow pod-like flower, and the less conspicuous hop trefoil, another member of the pea family. The clounded yellow may have only one brood in a year, laying its eggs on the upper side of clover leaves. The caterpillars, hatching in June, feed on clover and trefoils. The common blue prefers birdsfoot trefoil or the rest harrow, its eggs developing into green caterpillars with black heads.

May's whiteness is transformed by new colours as the days pass and nowhere more than in those gardens where man has 'improved' on nature, introducing exotic trees, shrubs and flowers. First man tames the wild and then changes it to his own taste. The garden of England is more than fruit and hops and an abundance of hedgerow flowers. The dry, sandy soils of the heaths of Surrey and Sussex, for so long a wasteland in terms of medieval agriculture and settlement, have been made so fertile as to transform private dreams into visions of paradise. Two plants above all others, introduced first in the seventeenth century, but even more abundantly in the nineteenth, suit such conditions, the rhododendron and the azalea. Bank upon bank of colour and scent, they form the framework that was once the function of yew and box hedges and brick walls.

Seeds of *Rhododendron arboreum* brought from the Himalayas in 1820 were adopted by Waterers of Surrey and became the first introduction of the now ubiquitous plant. Another forty-three species were introduced by Sir James Hooker in the 1850s to Kew and the search for new hybrid forms still continues. There are rhododendrons trained as trees, for example, at Squerryes near Westerham.

Behind the rhododendron banks are ranged the exotic trees, the evergreens and brilliant foliage from all over the world, sought by ardent botanists for the proud and affluent owners of estates. Fronting them are the flower beds, the lawns, the sunken gardens, the water gardens, the parterres, the knots, making a floral advance on the more formal gardens of the seventeenth century and the restrained passions of such gardeners as John Evelyn of Wotton in Surrey. Concepts such as his can still be admired, albeit rarely, in such places as Groombridge on the Kent–Surrey border, where he advised his friends, the Packers, on the layout of the formal terraced gardens to the north of the moated seventeenth-century mansion. House, moat and garden remain almost unchanged since that time.

Most of the gardens open to the public reach their visual climax in late May, so full of scent and colour that they leave you as drunk as a bee, meandering through a maze of paths. If I choose three parks for special mention, it is only partly for their horticultural eminence, but mostly for their geographical proximity, all grouped within a few miles in the central Weald, once the heart of the last medieval wilderness in the south, the frontier between the three counties. All three, Nymans, Sheffield Park and Borde Hill, are the result of the gardening passion of the Edwardian period, prompted and, in some cases, actually aided, by such pioneers of the new 'cottage' garden as Gertrude Jekyll and William Robinson. Robinson himself lived and worked at Gravetye in the same part of Sussex.

The overwhelming richness of Sheffield Park with everything from palm avenues to coffin juniper, from Japanese maples to Irish heath, is the work of A. G. Soames from 1909 to 1934. Apart from the hundreds of exotic trees that make the garden an arboretum, the emphasis is on rhododendrons, more than four hundred being planted out from a cross Soames planted in 1920. The framework of the garden, notably the four lakes which give it its visual focus and chief delight, was fashioned two centuries before by Capability Brown who began life in rural Northumberland and became one of the greatest landscape gardeners of his day. John Baker Holroyd, President of the Board of Agriculture and ardent improver, soon to be the 1st Earl of Sheffield, employed Brown to landscape his new estate. That first essay in the creation of water surfaces and open glades, punctuated by traditional trees, is still just recognisable. There is even evidence of the earlier landscape that preceded Brown in the shape of several ancient chestnut trees and oaks that stand humbly amongst the more stylish splendours. An avenue of palms runs alongside an oaky glade. Bluebells and common twayblades stand beneath a red-leaved sycamore. Marsh marigolds riot by the water's edge framed in the reflection of an import from China. It seems incongruous, but it works. After all, even the sweet chestnut was an exotic in its turn when the Romans introduced it. Most of the countryside is man-made or man-moulded, from the felling of the first tree to the grazing of the first grass. Sheffield Park is just one more stage in man's dominance of the landscape.

At Sheffield Park, the focus is the Middle Lake. At Nymans, the centre point is the burnt-out mansion. Its broken walls seem to heighten rather than detract from the wonder of wistaria and the enormous flowers of the magnolia grandiflora 'Goliath'. Six distinct gardens, the work, or should I say the art, of the Messel family and gardeners like James Comber and Cecil Nice, are held together in the natural frame of the parkland, a lime avenue, wild woods and open pastures embracing the smaller plots like treasured secrets. Some of the touches are magical, a weeping wych-elm standing on top of an artificial mound at the very centre of the heather garden. A Byzantine urn and an Italian loggia in a sunken garden fronted by one mass of forget-me-nots. Everywhere a liberal sprinkling of trees like the *Pieris forrestii* 'Wakehurst', a shrub which, not content with rows of white pendant flowers like large lilies-of-the-valley, produces new leaves of rich red hue. The Wakehurst appendage is a reference to the greatest of the gardens, Wakehurst Place, also in the Sussex Weald, administered by the Royal Botanical Gardens of Kew.

Nymans has a large collection of exotic dogwoods, their large flowers making the native dogwood of the chalk Downs look humble in the extreme. But there can be few final surprises as great as the ghost tree or the handkerchief tree near the car park which hangs its large white flowers down like rags tied to the branches; *Davidia viladriniana*, named after the French missionary who found the species in China and who also first reported the panda to European ears. Yet the variegated holly close by opens its white flowers with no less pride. Both Nymans and Sheffield Park are administered by the National Trust and are open for the summer months. There are many smaller private gardens open occasionally, sometimes, like Groombridge, only once a year under the National Garden Scheme. Some of the small gardens like Borde Hill a few miles from Sheffield Park have enough variety for one day's exploration. Mostly the result of planting by S. R. Clarke since the 1890s, Borde Hill claims one of the most comprehensive collections of rhododendron in private hands. The Long Dell and especially the azalea ring fronted by a tall Turkey oak are its highspots. The most extraordinary feature of all these gardens is the speed with which they have achieved their present maturity and abundance.

Such splendours need their antithesis. You cannot feed the senses like that every day. Only a handful of miles to the east of Sheffield Park lies the bleak, unenclosed heathland of Ashdown Forest with its more astringent beauty. Ashdown has witnessed every pressure for change and survived. At first a hunting area for early man, then traversed by Roman roads, it became the common land for the surrounding settlements, used for grazing and fuel. Then John of Gaunt held it as a private chase, stocked with deer and other beasts of the forest. Then it was overcut for fuel for the iron industry and suffered encroachments on every side, especially to the west by Crowborough for new enclosures and housing. Now, it is protected by a Board of Conservators and a Society of Friends of Ashdown Forest, an open space for the pleasure of motorists, riders, walkers, naturalists and students. Their very pressure makes its preservation as a site of special scientific interest the more difficult.

Its 6,400 acres of wet and dry heathland and woodland is developed on one of the oldest rock structures in the region, the infertile beds of the Ashdown Sands, the very core of the rocks that were uplifted into a great dome at the same time that the Alpine mountain chain was formed. To the north and to the south stand the two hill chains of Downs gazing across the Weald between them as if in memory of that far-off geological time when they were joined as one enormous deposition of chalk. Its geology is the basis of Ashdown, its flora the major interest. The management of the heath and woods is needed because of the decline of traditional commoners' practices. Fewer than fifty commoners still exercise their traditional rights of grazing livestock, of cutting trees for fuel and for house repairs, of cutting bracken for bedding. Parts of the heath are being allowed to revert to woodland and others are being cut to maintain the heather and more delicate flora. Drainage is carefully controlled so as to preserve the rarest floral habitats of all, the wet ghylls where plants such as the hay-scented fern and leafy liverwort have survived since the area was under tundra conditions on the edge of the ice sheet up to 10,000 years ago.

The sense of the wild is ever present with feral deer passing from cover to cover. They are mostly fallow, but a small herd of red deer is known and the occasional roe has been sighted. The fauna is abundant, if secretive, keeping clear of the many car-parks and the most trodden areas. Otters, foxes, badgers, stoats, moles, common shrews, hedgehogs, rabbits, dormice, harvest mice and woodmice, voles and American minks are all known to be within the forest bounds. Above soar the hobby and the kestrel on the lookout for the unwary rodent.

A long evening walk over this last outpost of the Wealden past is especially stimulating after the surfeit of exotic gardens. Black heather slopes down towards the dark silhouette of the South Downs, Gilbert White's 'vast range of mountains'. Young bracken fronds unfurl even in the recently burnt areas. A clump of Scots pine, planted only a century ago, look as if they belong to an immemorial landscape. Along the rides, dwarf furze and wild clary, milkwort and tormentil take advantage of the additional space and light. The wet ghylls are marked by lines of stunted alders and buckthorn. By the small waterfalls tumbling over the horizontal sandstone strata, mosses and liverworts enjoy the pockets of humidity.

A small heath butterfly rests on a grassy stem, almost invisible with its pale wings closed, two dots gleaming like watchful eyes. It moves gently up the stem where it will lay its small cluster of eggs. A stonechat, most characteristic bird of the open heath, calls drily from the top of a gorse bush. Everywhere the scattered hawthorn bushes bear their burden of blossom, a May beauty without peer.

CHAPTER 6

June

In 1629 Thomas Johnson of the City Company of Apothecaries took ten companions into rural Kent on an 'herbarising excursion', a serious forerunner of our more leisurely country pursuits. The wild flowers they sought were not just for the pleasure of their senses, but essential ingredients of their medicinal practices and, no doubt, the country walkers took some herbs home to improve the taste and smell of contemporary cooking.

At that time, the landscape had a much more open look than it does today, much of the original woodland cover having been cut over for building, for ships and fuel for iron furnaces, foundries and the widespread woollen industry. Most of the great houses had their own herb gardens, some persisting from the abandoned monastic sites, but the chief collecting area was on the chalk hills of the North

Downs. The June herbage is as varied as at any time of the year, with the last of the Spring flowers augmented by the new summer growth. Salad burnet, with its small globe of tiny red flowers, was used for staunching wounds and as an infusion against the gout. The small white pansy-type flower of eyebright was used to treat eye complaints and, appropriately, hay-fever. The yellow agrimony was sought for 'them that have naughty livers' and they were legion, according to Gerarde. Lungwort, with green spots on the leaves, was used for pulmonary complaints. The Latin name for self-heal is *Prunella*, an old name for sore throat.

Every herb to its use. The lovely pink centaury, that once cured the centaur, was good for intestinal troubles. Marjoram, one of the many varieties of mint making the grasslands odorous, was a regular standby in the kitchen. From the waysides and the hedgerows, mugwort, a herb associated with St John the Baptist, was gathered to fortify beer. By happy coincidence, the common St John's wort, another plant used to staunch bleeding, comes into flower around the saint's day on the 24th of the month. It made a rich, red oil used by the Crusaders. The plant is most abundant on lime-rich soils. Even the humble nettle, currently popular in the food-for-free movement, has been used since Roman times to treat rheumatism. White bryony, easily mistaken for travellers' joy until the distinctive leaves and the small, pale five-petalled flowers are recognised, was used for everything from hysteria to lumbago. Comfrey, too, was known as boneset, in great demand on medieval battlefields whilst Henry VIII was not averse to an infusion of broom against surfeit, a regular royal condition. The variety of potions and infusions makes our tea- and coffee-drinking age seem dull by comparison, yet the herbs still find their way into the thousands of pills we swallow in pursuit of good health. The very names sound like an incantation against illness, woundwort, lemon balm, feverfew, sweet Basil, bistort, angelica, opium and foxglove, thyme, dill and sage.

The charms can be invoked a hundredfold in the herb gardens that remain. One of the loveliest is at Sissinghurst, just one of the specialised gardens that fill the moated arena of a ruined Tudor house, restored and dramatically recreated in this century by Victoria Sackville-West and Harold Nicolson. Set inside a high hedge alongside an ancient nuttery, the garden can even boast a seat covered with chamomile, a cushion non-pareil. Between the aromatic garden and the old moat is a lawn of thyme. Sitting on that lawn once, overwhelmed with sight and smell, I watched a robin performing as adroitly as a fly-catcher, dashing from its perch on an overhanging oak bough to hover over the moat, grab a fly and hurtle back to its perch. Sissinghurst, even with all its visitors, keeps the atmosphere of a very private place. The gardens are small, each bound by brick walls, tall clipped hedges, unexpected arches opening up from one surprise to another, rose garden, to cottage garden, white garden to moat walk. The riotous informality, most noticeable in the cottage garden, is held in check in a formal neo-Tudor frame.

At Ightham, in the garden of the old vicarage, there are no such distractions from a collection of more than 200 herbs in a walled enclosure around a centre-piece of ancient apple trees and a back-cloth of massive vinestock growing into a greenhouse. Some of the herbs originated at near-by Seal, the collection of Mrs Brownlow, legendary enthusiast for the propagation of herbs. Row after row of herbs for kitchen or medicine chest rub shoulders or smells with more than a hundred planted just for their fragrance. There is a place where ring-a-ring of roses, pocket full of posies really make sense. My nose is not of the sharpest and one bouquet of rue drives out all other subtleties.

A small but efficient restoration can be seen at Hall Place in Bexley, one of several adventures in modern gardening in the appropriate setting of a Tudor mansion that has a medieval origin at least as old as the Black Prince, whose name is associated with the estate. The herbs are planted in parterres, surrounded by low-clipped box hedges which were fashionable with the Romans who preferred the box to the yew.

The pleasure of smells is exploited in the subscription garden at St Leonards on the Sussex coast, centre-piece of a nineteenth-century resort development by James Burton, whose bust stands in the gardens. The herbs are labelled in braille so that those who cannot enjoy sight can at least cherish the varied aromas. Such smells were once abundant even in places like Mitcham, famous for its physic gardens and lavender fields until building developments in the 1920s turned the Surrey fields into part of London's sprawl.

The enthusiasm for herbs is shown in the notes written for the flower festival at Challock Church in mid-Kent. Imagine the white interior of the church, set in an isolated downland valley, lit by June sunlight streaming through the south windows, the interior banked with herbs and flowers and an enormous bee bumbling by the west window of the south aisle. The moment was as enriching as the herbs themselves. Challock celebrates with herbs; Boughton Monchelsea with roses.

Any time of the year is a celebration in that well-tended church-yard lying beyond the finest medieval lychgate in the region. The path from the gate to the north porch is banked with rose of Sharon. South of the church, the ground falls to a panoramic view of the Weald. The yard is artfully fashioned into a series of steps with the happiest conjunction of cultivated and wild flowers. A wistaria is trained by the south wall to form a canopy over a group of graves. Below the churchyard wall, fallow deer graze in the park. A variety of trees line the enclosure including a fair-sized yew. June is for roses, the climax of the year in this hanging garden, maintained by the local people.

Fallow deer need their privacy. Observe them from a distance for the does are dropping their calves in bracken thickets. The atmosphere is as tender as the velvet on the newly formed antlers. Summer coats are looking sleek and richly speckled once more. The deer are most active in the early morning or in the cool of the late evening. There are still nine or more deer parks to choose from the small herd at Boughton to the public wilds of Royal Richmond. Young gorse, tender bracken, heather tips and bilberry are all in the diet. I watched a young buck literally walking on its hind legs for the best part of ten minutes, cropping the lower leaves of a lime tree. The leaves are sappy in June, the tree flowers at their best. Sometimes the deer severed an entire twig and brought it to the ground to graze more comfortably, the right foreleg rhythmically pawing the ground. Sweet chestnut, wych-elm and hornbeam were also savoured in that evening patrol, but the oak, though inspected thoroughly, was left untouched.

Deers are kept away from the inner gardens of the parks by high fences or ha-ha-ditches, but their tastes have extended with their range. There are hundreds of feral deer to be seen, many of them escapees from parks such as Uppark and Cowdray, Eastwell and Waldershare, which no longer maintain their traditional herds. Roe deer, one of the smallest of the species, roam freely through the woods and heathlands of West Sussex and Surrey and have developed a partiality for cultivated roses, much to the distress of enthusiastic gardeners. The deer tend to lay up during the day and carry out their sorties, early and late, creating havoc long before the owners are up and about. They are so adjusted to suburban living that they can plunder in broad daylight.

Roe and fallow were beasts of the chase as distinct from the red deer which were beasts of the forest, a royal monopoly. The finest herd of red still extant is in the royal park of Richmond. They too calve mostly in June and achieve the red-tinted coats that give them their name. Royal they are, antlers silhouetted against the improbable surrounds of leafy London suburbs and commuter cars roaring down the A3. Some of the finest specimens, descendants of the herd painted by Millais, are at Warnham Court in Sussex in the grounds of what is now a private school.

Herbage for the deer. Herbage for the apothecary. Roses for the church. June is the month of abundant growth, bursting out all over, as the song insists. Orchids are even more abundant than in May. The bees are so infatuated with the bee orchid that they try to mate with the flower and thereby assist pollination. By the end of the month, the pyramid orchid can be the most conspicuous flower in a dry chalk grassland. About seventeen species of orchid can be found in the nature reserve on Wye and Crundale Downs, some in the wooded copses, others on the steep slopes of the Devil's Kneading Trough, a dramatic coombe formed about ten thousand years ago at the close of the Ice Age, an area kept clear of public access. This is such a popular reserve, with its nature trail and a view as far as the power station at Dungeness that overuse is already a problem, erosion of the paths making deep white scars in the bedrock. In order to maintain the more delicate flora, like the orchids, attempts are made to eradicate coarser plants like the tor grass by mowing, by burning and by close cropping with sheep. There is an information centre with a warden usually in attendance in high summer.

Grasses, as every hay-fever sufferer knows, reach their climax in June. Of all the plants, they are the most important in the maintenance of our food supplies. They cover a greater area than any other plant. Even on a simple patch of chalk as Coulsdon Down, the nature trail laid out by the local authority introduces at least sixteen grasses. With names almost as evocative as the herbs, such as Yorkshire fog, sweet vernal grass, crested dog's tail, small quaking grass and red fescue, they deserve more attention than we usually give them.

Arthur Young enthused about the quality of the Sussex grasses when he was writing his famous reports on English agriculture in the early years of the nineteenth century. 'It is the herbage of the Downs which renders the flavour of the mutton so exquisitely fine, the flesh so firm and the wool so excellent.' The decline of grazing has changed the character of the grasslands. The grasses which grow most abundantly on waste ground and neglected pastures are not the most important for the June hay-cut or the later summer grazing. Farmers select and sow the most nutritious, such as the fluffy topped Yorkshire fog, the trim crested dog's tail, the erect timothy. Two of the finest grasses, from a farming point of view, come from an unexpected area, the heavy clay soils of the Wealden plain, especially south-west of Ashford around Bethersden. The wild white clover (not strictly a grass) and the perennial rye-grass dominate the pastures there and are often found together.

In growing trials carried out in the 1880s the wild white clover from the Bethersden area was found to give maximum returns; treated with basic slag, close cropped by sheep, the clover yielded more seed in August than any other species. The clover produced small plants with a broad spread over the ground, improved by treading or grazing. Now selected seeds of the Kentish white clover and the Kentish perennial rye-grass are cultivated as an arable crop.

The first clover used in the south-east was introduced from the Netherlands by Sir Richard Weston in about 1645. He lived at Sutton Place, one of the finest Tudor mansions in Surrey. Many of the bricks in the façade of the house bear the initials RW, recalling the founder of the family fortunes in Henry VIII's reign. The later Sir Richard was a pioneer agriculturist who wrote directions for the cultivation of the 'great clover' which led to a rapid expansion of its use. The hay fields along the valley of the river Wey near Sutton Place are still amongst the best in the region.

Hay-making is not as poetic as it once was with scythe and rake, but infinitely more labour-saving. The mechanised cutters race round the big fields with bronzed drivers taking advantage of the sun. Grasses and flowers fall before the cutting edge with clouds of dust and seeds and pollen puffing into the sultry air. Then the balers join the procession, plonk-plonk, plonk-plonk, wrapping the hay into neat blocks with minimum ceremony. The dry seasons of recent years have made hay a precious commodity, needed even in early summer to supplement scarce feed. One farmer at Headcorn, again in the Kent clay country, has made a first cut as early as March and found a second profitable cut ready in the traditional June. This same farmer won a world prize for his wild white clover.

The rich hay fields around Headcorn and Bethersden occur on one of the largest areas of level land in the region, one of the few places where it seems right to use the word 'plain'. Whether seen from the top of the tower at Sissinghurst or from the crest of the downs on the nature reserve above Wye, the land spreads out as flat as a palm. The origin of its clay deposits was a great lacustrine flat, the so-called Wealden lake that existed before the formation of the chalk hills. One of the geological delights of that lake was the presence of beds of fresh-water snails. The fossilised remains of those snails can be found in pathways, in walls and bridges, or used as decorative marble in churches and the fireplaces of mansions like Knole. Thousands of small rectangular extraction pits pock the plain giving a liberal supply of pond water for stock and a bonus for the country walker for those ponds supply a haven of insect life in the hot summer days. Skaters and water-boatmen dash about over the common duck-weed and a large water-beetle executes his forceful breast stroke just below the surface. Brilliant blue emperor dragonflies dance as erratically as helicopters. Two large red damselflies lock together, head to tail, in their complicated mating ritual and fly in tandem. As they come to rest on a fallen willow twig, the male twists his body into a rising arc. The eggs fall into the water.

One of the most prolific displays of pond life was in one of the more evil looking hollows, the stagnant water stained with the rusty metal of old cars, with a rich edging of plantain, flags, loose-strife, bittersweet and foxglove. A dip into the pond brought out the most abundant harvest of larvae and maggots and mites all making their tiny contribution to the life-pattern of what seemed at first sight a most unpromising habitat. The bigger marble extraction ponds, often found near medieval farmhouses, attract the larger aquatic animals and a shadowy fringe of anglers hiding under rainbow umbrellas.

An even more remarkable group of ponds is found in artificial hollows high up on the South Downs, giving a much needed water source on the dry chalk hills. The origin of the dew-ponds and their mode of replenishment are much debated topics. Some are certainly as old as the Celtic field systems, but others have been created in recent times, complete with concrete lining and plastic sheets in place of the old puddled clay. Traditionally called dew-ponds, due to the belief that they were filled by the condensation of dew, many have been empty for years and others filled in or lost to the plough. Even along by such a popular beauty spot as Ditchling Beacon there are ponds full enough to support water crowsfoot and water forget-me-not.

Ponds on the whole are a neglected asset doomed to extinction by colonisation by plants or by the thoughtless rubbish of our society. The village pond is almost as much a fossil relic of a bygone age as the snails in the Bethersden marble. Yet the ducks still assert their territory at Goudhurst, much to the consternation of small children, the swans look fierce in the yellow waters of Matfield and a succession of dry years may bring the pond back to favour. There is a particularly murky pond by the roadside at Warlingham, but it still had its quota of three small boys in statuesque vigil grasping their home-made fishing rods, the personification of optimism on a fine June day.

The cleanest, clearest water is found in the springs that break out at the base of the chalk, a rock that stores water like a sponge. The line of springs is common to the vales that front the North and South Downs, favoured sites for farm and village since Roman times and perhaps even earlier. Ponded up, the springs make superb watercress beds. Some of the best are at the northern extremity of the chalk country as it reaches towards the Thames estuary at Teynham. According to one writer on agriculture, the first cultivated watercress, as distinct from the wild variety, was grown at Springhead near Northfleet. It may be just a coincidence that the beds are not far from the old naval dockyards and that the cress, rich in vitamin C, was useful in the treatment of scurvy. The biggest beds I know are on the Tillingbourne near Albury in Surrey, where the water, a tributary of the Wey, flows from the sandstone strata.

Whether on pond or river, the anglers become expectant after the 16th of the month when the coarse fishing season starts. They are not the only fishermen along the marshland channels. Patrolling the same channels with easy wingbeat are the terns. Heads watchfully down, forked tails spread wide, they take a purposeful line. Then the tail twitches, the wings thrust down and the small body moves sharply upwards before plummeting down, recovering with a frenzy of wings just as the beak breaks the water surface and rises with its prey, circling the banks to regain height before returning to the patrol.

Much has changed in the marshes since we saw them in mid-winter. Choosing the same starting points, the church at Lower Halstow or Hoo or Teynham, we can follow the sea walls which were then slippery with mud and snow flurries. Now the earth banks are cracking with drought. In January, dusk fell early on the screams of wildfowl. Now in the long, lazy evenings the tall reeds rustle with the activity of hundreds of unseen birds. Warblers are nesting and feeding, flashing into view on sudden errands. Then a cuckoo flies sedately over the nests on a hawthorn bush, before dropping into the reeds, amongst the warblers which foster its strange offspring. Wagtails and reed buntings feed more conspicuously, darting along the dykes. A pair of lapwing mob an errant crow and a heron stalks through the shallow water searching for eels. Mallard and shelduck wheel in from the estuarine mud-flats and a great crested grebe paddles along with its chicks on its back.

Quite apart from the bird-life, there is the specialised flora: sea aster, sea purslane, sea-lavender, sea-beet, sea spurrey and the aromatic sea wormwood. Glasswort and eel grass emerge greenly from the mud, each plant to its own zone.

The same abundance, with the addition of the rarer species like bitterns and bearded tits, occurs in the official reserves like Stodmarsh with marsh frogs croaking a bubbly song. A less welcome sound, at least to local inhabitants, is the loud mating call of the Hungarian laughing frog introduced into Romney Marsh in the 1920s and now prolific enough to keep the human residents awake at night.

An excess of water produces dramatic results in any landscape, but especially in areas where surface water is otherwise rare. The contrast can be studied in all its microcosmic clarity at Hothfield Common, one of the last remaining areas of true heath in Kent and in the same general area as Bethersden and Wye that we have already visited. Hothfield differs from both, being a local nature reserve at the eastern end of the greensand ridge, the last assertion of the sandstone rocks before they plunge beneath the plain. The dry heath is typical, dominated by heather and bracken with the occasional birch, oak and clumps of pine with gorse and hawthorn bushes, and a copse of beech and chestnut on higher slopes, furnace hot in summer, where the grass snakes and occasional adder bask in the sun. Fire rages across the dry heath periodically, the heat stored in the peat and accumulated litter of dead bracken being fanned by strong winds and high temperatures into a smouldering mass. But the importance of the reserve lies not in its dry heath which can be seen to a much larger extent in Surrey and West Sussex, but in its low-lying bogs caused by impeded drainage. The nature trail leads from the roadside car-park not far from the A20 through the beech woodland down to a causeway built by volunteers that leads across the largest of the bogs. In late June it is smothered with common spotted orchids and bog asphodels. An occasional marsh orchid and common twayblade lurks in the shade, with ragged robin, a plant once common that seems to get rarer every year.

The floor of the bog is cushioned with hummocks of sphagnum moss brightened with the extraordinary leaves, like red hairy purses, of sundew growing on the moss. The attraction of sundew is fatal to the insects that visit for it is a carnivorous plant. Its sparkle is due to a sticky fluid which traps the prey. The delicate leaves fold over like tentacles to complete the catch. As the sphagnum hummocks grow upwards with the access of moisture, they drain out and dry enough for cross-leaved heath to grow. It is flowering already. So is the milkwort which seems to thrive on every soil from dry chalk to wet marsh. Wetter patches are marked by a display of cotton grass that wouldn't be out of place on a Pennine moor.

Amongst the abundant moths, flies and butterflies is the unusual orange underwing moth which flies by day and feeds especially on the polytrichum moss. The birch tree is a rapid coloniser at Hothfield and spreads into the wet zones from the surrounding slopes. In doing so, it dries out the bog and changes the conditions that support the rarer plants. So the birch has to be cut back. In the lower bog, birch has been controlled so as to maintain a continuous cover of heather, a rarity in Kent. Several soil pits have been cut so as to expose the soil horizons. But the best intentions of the conservation corps are sometimes thwarted by thoughtless acts of vandalism, the destruction of the causeway, the occasional match or fire that can turn the heath with summer temperatures of nearly 40°C into an inferno. One of the characteristic birds of Hothfield is the yellowhammer still singing in the heat of June when most other birds have long fallen into summer silence.

Gazing at bog asphodels or dipping into ponds are amongst the cooler pleasures of the midsummer month, but the farming round has one of the tougher jobs at hand, the shearing. The van arrives and the contract men jump out, set up tent and tackle in the shade of an oak, start the donkey engine into action and keep the medicaments handy. The sheep, especially the yearlings, stampede fearfully in their pens in the corner of a Wealden field. Then the first ewe is taken, sprawled on its back, one human leg carefully placed across the woolly body so as to cause minimum movement then the beast seems to freeze with fear as the shears roll up the stomach, then work up one flank after the other until the fleece hangs like a shaggy coat. Round the neck, down the back. In four or five minutes, its all over. The ewe stands up, subdued, bewildered, then bounds off uncertainly to its summer freedom, shorn of its pride. The men work quickly, deftly, silently, unwilling to stop for a chat, for time is money. One nick of the flesh may need dressing and that takes time, so speed is matched with skill. The hands greasy with wool, hot with sweat, have to be patient and steady.

Some shepherds still shear their own flocks, but most are done by bands of itinerant shearers and the sound of the donkey engine is as much part of the scene as the protests of the sheep. The best of the wool clip, the long staple, comes from the Romney or Kent sheep. The Southdown for mutton and lamb, the Romneys for wool. Many a monastery was made rich by its flocks. At first the wool was exported to the continent, controlled by the Staple at Canterbury, but from the reign of Edward III the weavers came to the southeast, to Sandwich, to Canterbury and especially to Cranbrook in the Weald of Kent. When Good Queen Bess came on her royal progress through Surrey and Kent, she rode sometimes on carpets of Kentish broadcloth laid down on village streets for her pleasure.

The profits of the wool trade built many a church tower and mansion. Hundreds of timber-framed houses bear the name of the Weavers, the most famous being by the Stour at Canterbury. The finest architectural reminders of the woollen industry are the cloth halls, the houses of affluent merchants, as at Smarden, Headcorn and Cranbrook in Kent and at Wonersh in Surrey, superb timbered houses with every embellishment that timber could provide. Some mill sites, like those along the Len south of Maidstone, were fulling mills. The cleansing of the wool needed two main materials, a lot of water and a supply of Fullers' earth to extract the grease. That special earth was happily found along the greensand ridge, at Leeds and Boxley. It is still worked in a huge quarry at Nutfield in

Surrey, a fine light clay as soft as plasticine when rolled between the fingers.

The fruit blossom is over, the hops are climbing steadily up the strings aiming to reach the top traditionally by midsummer day and the soft fruit farmer is ready for the first picking. The traditional Sussex fare for Whitsun celebrations used to be roast veal and gooseberry pie, but a lot depended on the date of that moveable feast. The veal was secure, but the gooseberries might be late. The country lanes are placarded with the signs of strawberries. Pick your own, says the inviting legend. Even before Surrey celebrates the Wimbledon fortnight, the fields around the penumbra of the metropolis begin to yield their succulent fruit, like a red halo inviting the townsman to country pursuits.

The best of the market gardens were started by the same Flamands who brought their skills to the woollen industry and stayed to turn the south bank of the Thames into fruitfulness. Fast modern transport has enabled farmers far from London to pander to the city's sweet tooth and strawberries are grown as far afield as Romney. The highest sunshine rate, however, is found along the Sussex coast and this, together with fertile soil and level ground, has stimulated the glasshouse farming behind Worthing. More than a quarter of all the soft fruits of England are grown in the south-east. Long nylon nets like enormous sausages curl across the fields creating their own climates, enabling ambitious farmers to grow their fruits out of season. Gooseberries and strawberries, make a succulent prelude to raspberry and loganberry, blackcurrants overlapping with the first of the cherries. A notable antithesis to the 'pick-your-own' fashion is the enormous machine in the fields around Marden, gobbling up blackcurrants like a giant vacuum cleaner.

More and more farmers are encouraging visitors, not only by the prospect of picking fresh fruit straight from the bush but by farm open days with trails laid out throughout the buildings and fields. Each year one Kent farm is chosen for an open day, but many farmers make their own private arrangements. Old farm implements and machinery tucked away in the barns attract as much attention as the growing crops. These are the gentle days between hay harvest and the main harvest when time seems to stand still and leisure stretches with the light. The townsman is happy to return to his rural roots.

CHAPTER 7

July

The wooden signpost on Bignor Common in West Sussex is as dramatic as its setting. One arm bears the name 'Londinium', pointing north-eastwards across the Weald; another points south-wards to 'Regnum', the Roman city of Chichester. Standing on a burial mound of even greater antiquity than the Roman sites, the signpost stands at a crossroads of ancient tracks. East and west runs the Ridgeway, now followed by the South Downs Way. At Bignor Common it crosses the Roman Stane Street which linked Chichester with London. For the walker there is an embarrassment of riches. In a month named after a Roman emperor, the route to the south beckons most strongly.

The wayside flora dons an imperial mantle with many variations of purple, knapweed, dwarf thistle, red bartsia, scabious, hemp agrimony, willowherb. Even amongst the encroaching scrub, Stane Street is clearly defined, raised on an embankment, its surface packed with flints. After a mile on the Common, it marches through cornfields past Gumber Corner with gnarled ash and hazel along its banks until it drops into the dark shadows of Earthem Wood. The ranks of the new forestry plantations are as strict in their alignment as the Street itself. South of the conifer ranks is an extensive area of older deciduous woodland with tall beeches and self-sown ash, shaws of spindle, thorn and elder lining the paths towards the village of Slindon. The Slindon beeches, like Stane Street, are owned by the National Trust.

In July the forest rides hold the possibilities of rare encounters, perhaps the glimpse of a roe deer or a muntjac slipping through the shades. Watch carefully for a high-flying butterfly with black and white markings breaking across the sunbeams as they penetrate the forest canopy, the white admiral. Sometimes it settles on the bulky purple heads of hemp agrimony which grows prolifically on the disturbed ground on either side of the Roman track. At rest, it is inconspicuous. When it flies, it is unmistakable. Its image is frequently seen in Sussex for it appears on the signs of nature reserves controlled by the Sussex Naturalists' Trust. An older generation of entomologists called it the 'white admirable', a much better name. Even more suitable is the French, *le petit sylvain*, the little woodlander.

The natural habitat of the white admiral is the damp oak woodland of the Weald. The plant essential to its life cycle is the honeysuckle which thrives in the undergrowth, tangled up with the bracken. The larva winters in a hibernaculum formed by a leaf of honeysuckle drawn into an enclosing capsule by delicate silken threads. The eggs are laid in July. The yellow larva, covered with red prickles, evolves into this most graceful of fliers.

It is no accident that the Sussex naturalists have adopted the butterfly, now a comparative rarity, as their emblem, for it is in that county that some of the best examples of nature oak woodland survive. Oak will grow on any soil in the south-east and represents what botanists call the climax vegetation. The oak dominated the whole region before man undertook the clearance of the forest. The early people who erected the tumuli on Bignor Common looked down on oak forest. The oak is still the dominant tree in both Sussex and Kent, according to forestry statistics. There are two major species of oak: the pedunculate, *Quercus robur*, the English oak, wide-spreading with massive twisted branches lowering to the ground, the acorns in pairs on prominent stalks, thrives on heavy clay soils typical of the Low Weald; the sessile or durmast oak, with a tendency to straighter branches and more upright stance, prefers the lighter soils that are found on the sandstone ridges of the High Weald. The acorns tend to be shorter than on the *robur*. Many intermediate forms exist and identification is often uncertain.

Arthur Young, the traveller and writer on agricultural affairs, was very ambivalent in his attitude to the Sussex oak. The merit of its timber was not in doubt. He reported that the naval shipyards of Portsmouth, producing the wooden walls of England for defence of the coast against the French, insisted on Sussex oak. Yet Young called it the 'weed that springs up in every protected spot. If a field were sown with furze only.' he wrote, 'and livestock excluded, the ground in the course of a few years would be covered with young oaks, without any trouble or expense of planting.' Despite the fact that 2,000 mature oaks were needed to build one first-rate ship-of-the-line, Young estimated that Sussex alone could supply all the Navy's requirements. He preferred corn, which was five times more profitable in his estimation. The woods surrounding the fields prevented the corn from drying properly for harvest and were 'nurseries for insects and vermin'.

Young would find many a farmer and even forester to echo his words today. The Forestry Commission declares that it loses money by planting oaks. Fashions change. Economics change. The curved timbers that supplied the frames of medieval houses and church roofs and the sides of ships are anathema today. The timber market wants fast-growing, straight softwoods that can be grown like an industrial crop. So the traditional oak territory is invaded by spruce and larch and pine.

The loss of the oak is the loss of nature's variety, Arthur Young's 'insects and vermin'. For the oak is host to more species than any other tree, more than 300 according to naturalists. There are times when I would like to see Young's assertion tested and a vast area of the Weald enclosed and left alone just to see how long it would take for the oaks to reclaim the area. But the vast forest stretching from Hampshire to the Kent coast must be left to the imagination fed by the evidence of history, the *Sylva Anderida* of Roman times recorded in hundreds of place-names. We have to be content with smaller wonders such as the Cut and the Mens near Bedham in West Sussex. Only three miles west of Stane Street where it strides through Pulborough, the Mens is an area of oak woodland about 350 acres in extent stretching in patches for about two miles downslope from the village of Bedham to Wisborough Green that has been saved by the efforts of the Sussex Trust for Nature Conservation.

The word 'Mens' is unusual and may be related to the German word *gemeine* meaning 'common', the common land of the manor of Bedham. As a common used in the past for swine pastures and fuel gathering, it may not always have been as dense as it now is. Quite apart from all the familiar uses, oak from this area was also used in the medieval glass-making industry, which existed just to the north in the area around Wisborough Green and Chiddingfold. Nevertheless, the Mens is probably as near to the aboriginal forest as we shall find. I had my first sight of it from a narrow, tree-shaded lane winding its way up from Fittleworth in such a haphazard way that the lane itself seemed lost, aiming for no special destination. I went through Bedham, one of my objectives, without seeing the hamlet, partly because the place was hidden in the forest, but mostly because the view was so spectacular.

Mature beech trees are lovely in themselves, but when they act as the frame for a vista that seems to go on and on to a distant horizon without a building in sight, then they are compelling. The Mens looks so natural. We know it isn't. There is hardly a natural landscape left in the south-east. But the place seems untouched by man's incursions. Even the farms and hamlets still bear the marks of their origins as forest clearings, the dens and hursts of the Saxon swine pastures, with names like Hawkhurst and Battlehurst. Crimbourne, on the lower ground, must be one of the finest farm groups in the whole region, not a building out of place or time.

For the most part, the Mens is rough and dense and thorny and damp. Beneath the canopy of oak, beech and occasional hornbeam is an underwood of holly, yew, hazel, hawthorn, dogwood and crab apple. Both the spindle tree and the wild service are present, sure indicators of ancient woodland cover. The fallen trees are left to rot, the decaying wood being home for woodpeckers and nut-hatches, for insects, lichens and fungi. About a quarter of the living organisms of the forest are found in dead wood. Tidying up the forest reduces its ecological interest. So the Mens is left to its natural devices.

Even in the dry summers which have been a feature of the last decade, the oak woodland retains a high humidity and encourages plants such as the hay-scented fern to grow. Here, too, the white admiral butterfly may be seen, together with the purple emperor and the purple hairstreak, both being at home in these conditions. Feral deer wander through, augmenting the sense of the wild. The Mens is a very special place, a reminder of what England was like before the trees fell before the axe.

The best place to find out more about the Mens and other such sites is Woods Mill, near Henfield, also in West Sussex. The restored water-mill is the headquarters of the Sussex Naturalists' Trust and a very well-equipped information centre. Behind the mill is a small nature reserve on the flat Wealden clay, typical oak country, with a short nature trail laid out so cunningly that the area seems much bigger than it really is. The outstanding trees are water-lovers like white willow, black poplar and alder interspersed between an area of coppiced birch and hazel. Goldfinches, redpolls and siskins feeding on the seeds are supplemented by nesting boxes to attract great tits, blue tits and tree-creepers. The lake, an acre in extent, has kingfishers and martins visiting as well as resident moorhens, mallard and coots, with eel, carp, tench and golden orfe amongst the underwater life.

The lake shore and the adjacent canal banks are riots of summer colour with loosestrife, hemp agrimony, reed mace, willowherbs growing tall and, on the water surface, lillies and amphibious bistort. Generally, the flora is remarkably varied, including orchids, and all carefully labelled for easy identification. An additional feature of the flora is a garden near the mill commemorating William Borrer who lived at Henfield from 1782 until 1862. In his long lifetime he amassed a collection of more than 6,000 species of plants, many of them gathered locally. After a long absence, the white admiral was seen on the reserve in the 'butterfly summer' of 1976, together with such rarities as the white-letter hairstreak feeding on bramble blossom. There is even a pond-dip supplied to encourage the youngest embryo naturalists. The display of materials relating to the many nature reserves in Sussex is as attractive and imaginative as the reserve itself.

JULY

Sussex is one of the most wooded counties in Englands, well above the national average, with about 20 per cent of its surface covered, mostly in West Sussex and the Weald. There are several small patches of oak woodland to be studied such as the one hundred acres of Nap Wood, south of Tunbridge Wells which was bequeathed to the National Trust in 1966 by Mr Robert Courthope. Courthope is a name to conjure with when talking of oaks for the Courthope family owned extensive estates on the Sussex–Kent border. From Whiligh came the oak timbers for the House of Commons in 1832 and again for the rebuilding after the Second World War. The Sprivers estate at Horsmonden, another Courthope estate, has recently been given to the National Trust. Before the library was dispersed, I was fortunate enough to see a diary kept by Alexander Courthope, an eighteenth-century owner, who recorded every tree he planted, the exotic imports such as the two larches still by the front lawn and the white poplars, fashionable in his time, but especially the chestnut trees he planted 'raised from the nut'. Very few great oaks remain at Sprivers.

Nap Wood, in contrast, looks natural, yet most of the trees are only 130 years old, mostly replanted in the nineteenth century. On a steep hillside running from sandstone ridge down to clay vale, the reserve is dominated by oaks though the best individual trees are beech with a thick understorey of rowan and holly. Despite Arthur Young's claim about the weed of the Weald, the oak is regenerating so poorly that the Naturalists' Trust is planting three-year old seedlings to assist the process. A circular nature trail is open to visitors throughout the summer on Sundays. The most important flora lies beyond the public area on the low, wet ground where the iron concentrates from the sub-soil rocks encourages golden saxifrage, large bittercress and march violets, as well as a variety of ferns and liverworts.

Another 'tiny remnant of the vast forest of Anderida', to quote the publicity pamphlet, lies in East Sussex, south of the moated priory of Michelham. Abbot's Wood covers 800 acres, most of it being new softwood plantations, but oak has been planted with Norway spruce. The spruce will give a cash return comparatively quickly, leaving the ground clear for the oaks to mature and yield their hard timber in turn. Softwoods include the western hemlock, Japanese larch, Douglas fir, cedar and Scots pine. Along the rides are the expected colours of ragwort, scabious, tormentil and slender thistle, but this wood is also the location of one of the rarest of the region's plants, the spiked rampion, possibly introduced as a herb by the Augustinian monks and now growing wild. The pond in the wood was dug in 1965 to supply water for fire-fighting as well as to attract birds, but the ponds on the priory site itself, such as the Cardinal's stews, are medieval, being used for fish-farming. An extensive car-park on the road from Wilmington and ample public tracks make this one of the most accessible of the many Wealden remnants.

Dene Park, or Claygate, is part of the Commission forest around Shipbourne on the Wealden clay in Kent. Many of the conifers have made poor growth on the sticky yellow soil since planting began in the 1930s, but the oak and beech have done well. The forest trail, laid out for the public, threads through 200 of the 3,000 acres. Across the road from the public car park, on the Tonbridge road, is an especially fine stand of oaks, tall and slender, quite different in aspect from the Mens, showing the effect of management which has timber production in mind rather than natural amenity.

One of the most important forests of all lies in the very opposite corner of the region, just to the north of Canterbury. The forests of the Blean, a national nature reserve, were part of the great estates of the Archbishops, so that names like Church Woods abound and farms often bear the name 'court', a sure link with the ecclesiastical past. The woods, though broken into blocks by roads and occasional clearances, stretch for the best part of ten miles. A small block of one hundred acres, Ellenden Wood, is controlled by the Kent Naturalists' Trust. Much of the forest is managed on behalf of the ecclesiastical commissioners with the usual conifer plantations, but many areas of oak woodland remain, together with chestnut coppice which does especially well on the London clay soils. The clay is a younger formation, geologically speaking, than the Wealden clay, but shares some of its characteristics, with a high moisture-holding capacity and high mineral content. Elsewhere the London clay has been cleared for farming, but the low plateau of the Blean, for historic reasons, has been left as part of the halo of forests that encircle Canterbury.

On the higher ground beech becomes dominant but, as with all long-established woodlands, there is a variety of trees, including the hornbeam, the whitebeam, birch, wild cherry, crab apple, holly and in one small area the largest number of wild service trees I have seen anywhere in the region. The wild service has aroused a great deal of interest in recent years due to its increasing rarity. Within the Weald it is known as the Chequers tree and suggestions have been made that the many Chequers inns and Chequers farms may mark old sites of the tree. There are some fine examples planted in an avenue near Bethersden, as tall as the other trees, but most examples are small and inconspicuous, reminiscent of the whitebeam to which it is related. Its berries, which are already green and brown in late July, can be added to whisky. Taken with sugar and brandy they make a dessert to remember. When they are nearly rotten they can be eaten direct and were on sale in Covent Garden even in the last century. In one part of the Blean I saw dozens of seedlings and saplings growing by a path, the tree showing that it will regenerate when given suitable conditions.

The Blean is the type of place to expect the white admiral, but it has not been recorded there in recent years. The purple hairstreak is in residence together with so many other butterflies, moths and flies that a bright, sunny July day offers every inducement to sit down in a clearing and watch their activities. The bramble is the chief attraction. In little more than half an hour I saw at least twelve different butterflies in a bramble-filled clearing, nearly one-fifth of the total species in the country. East Kent, being so close to the continent, attracts many summer visitors and, though each butter-fly has its own special flora for feeding and for egg-laying, the pinky-white flowers of the blackberry seem to attract more than any other plant. For the non-specialist, the fascination is in the conjunction of colour, peacock butterfly resting on the golden heads of St John's wort, marbled whites on the purple heads of knapweed. Six-spot burnets, red-winged, glowing like copper, alight on the slender thistle. Red admirals and tortoiseshells take turns on the teasel. Yellow brimstone prefers the bramble, followed in succession by small heaths, green-veined whites, skippers and ringlets with their smokey wings. The marbled white is known locally as the half-mourner because of its black and white markings, but those mark-ings can vary in parts of Kent from almost pure white to black. Identification is difficult without a close inspection of the insect. Unfortunately, there are always those who inspect too closely, the hunters and collectors armed with chloroform and bottles who cream off the rarer species for their private gain.

A warm, sunny July will being out butterflies everywhere, on open downs as much as in woodlands. Wherever there is a clump of stinging nettles there may be a writhing infestation of black caterpillars of the peacock butterfly. The nettle is the chief breeding site for many butterflies such as the red admiral and small tortoise-shell. The yellow brimstone has a more specialised taste, for purging buckthorn, a small tree which can tolerate chalk soils, but is also found on wet heaths. The ragwort, common plant of every waste-land and woodland edge, is host to the tiger-striped caterpillars of cinnabar, one of the tiger moths, frequently seen in July. This the caterpillar is poisonous to most birds and the plant is noxious, too, an unwholesome but colourful combination. Such noxiousness is helpful to survival for even a small bird like the blue tit can eat up to seven hundred caterpillars in a day.

Individual oaks of immense girth and legendary age survive not so much in woodlands as in enclosed parks, such as Knole, Lulling-stone and Stonewall. Two deer parks, Petworth and Cowdray, the former still retaining its deer herd, stand close to the old wood-land of the Mens, affording a conveniently close geographical comparison. The oaks stud the landscape like sentinels, often bent and burnt by storms, for the oak is more vulnerable than other trees to lightning. One of the finest monarchs stands on the boun-dary of the churchyard at Headcorn in the Kentish clay vale, hollow as a pipe, propped up but still in leaf. The greatest girth of 11.28m. belongs to the 'Majesty' oak in Fredville Park in East Kent in the chalk country.

Oaks are not the only leviathans. The largest ash tree I have ever seen stands again on a churchyard perimeter, at Boughton Aluph on the North Downs near Wye, though there are others nearly as large in Godinton Park, Chilham and Cobham, all in Kent. The countryside would bear a very different face if people had not planted trees for their sheer pleasure, as an amenity. They planted them, knowing that only future generations would see the full mature glory of the trees. The extensive beech woodlands of the Goodwood Estate were planted mostly in the eighteenth and nine-teenth centuries using conifers as a nurse crop, a forestry practice still followed today. The 3rd Duke of Richmond added a thousand cedars of Lebanon to his plantations, together with cork oaks, some of which have survived two centuries of change. Most of the famous beech clumps like Chanctonbury and the Knockholt beeches in Kent were the result of planting by individual landowners, partly inspired by John Evelyn's impassioned plea for trees, *Sylva*,

published in 1664 which led to a massive reafforestation in a countryside that had been overcut for centuries. With estates in Albury,
Surrey and family possessions in Sussex, Evelyn wrote at a time when
the felling of trees for ships and iron furnaces was at its height. The
forges of Abinger Hammer were near Albury and his own family
were involved in the manufacture of gunpowder. His book was not
just a eulogy but a practical guide for foresters. The Evelyn name
still appears on the estate signs south of Albury on the forested slopes
of Leith Hill.

Beech mast and acorns were the staple diet of the swine herds
penetrating the early Weald and both, unfortunately, are regarded
highly by the grey squirrel. The young trees suffer especially, both
by debarking and deformation due to attacks on the young growing
shoots. This, on top of the estimated loss of 95 per cent of the acorns
to squirrels and wood pigeons, makes natural regeneration difficult
and hardwoods so unprofitable that some landowners give up.
These depredations by squirrels are especially common in early
summer.

The grey squirrel is a comparatively new invader and has upset
the ecological balance of woodland. Introduced from the Americas
in the 1870s, groups were released into the countryside in several
areas of the south-east, as far apart as Richmond Park in Surrey
and Sandling in East Kent. They spread rapidly at the expense
of the native red squirrel, a smaller species. In the 1900s red
squirrels were still common throughout the region, but the only
record now is in a limited zone between Dover and Folkstone. A
forester can erect a tall fence against deer and other grazing stock,
but he cannot cover a forest to keep the squirrels out. Selective
shooting makes little difference for the grey has two breeding seasons,
in early spring and early summer. Yet the observation of squirrels
can be a great source of interest and a much-needed touch of the
wild in an increasingly tamed landscape. Quite apart from their
gross feeding habits which can send cascades of discarded husks
and twigs and even pine cones on an unsuspecting walker, they
display a great variety of activities and calls.

On a July day in a beechwood at Chevening in north-west Kent,
I watched a grey squirrel advance towards a fallen twig. It grasped
the twig and then tumbled head over heels. Leaping to one side
it pounced back on the twig then lay on its back and lacerated the
wood with its back paws before running off with many a sportive

twist and turn. It ran up a beech trunk, pausing occasionally to emit harsh cries with its tail oscillating up and down. In the safety of a higher fork, it shouted like a jay, changing to a high-pitched cry with the tip of its curled tail vibrating violently. Finally, with a few mournful notes, just like the peewits in the adjacent pasture, it lolloped off, chattering and screaming in apparent anger. Often, at dusk, I have been puzzled by unusual bird songs only to find that they were part of the squirrel's repertoire.

From many of its famous viewpoints, like Bignor Common, Leith Hill or Blackdown, the Weald gives the visual impression of an essentially wooded landscape, due especially to the abundant hedgerow timber that surrounds the small enclosed fields. The pastoral tradition in the forest clearings survives although grain crops are increasing their acreage every year. The medieval pigs have given way to sheep and cattle. One of the cattle breeds found in the Weald has a pedigree as old as the forest. The Red Sussex, sleek, mahogany brown, is a descendant of the wild oxen that were bred as draught animals, pulling carts and heavy ploughs. Only they could cope, dragging the great Kentish turn-wrist plough through the heavy clay soils, soup in winter, cement in summer.

The Sussex is the oldest of purely English breeds and appeared at the first Smithfield Show in 1799. It is now having something of a revival as a beef animal, though modern breeding has substantially changed its characteristics. Its merit lies in its ability to fatten up on comparatively poor pastures, and recent dry summers have produced many of those. Of course, it enjoys stall-feeding and the lush riverside pastures, but it can outwinter safely. To the farm economist it has a low-cost input. In other words, it can eat sparse coarse grasses and still produce good beef when the time comes. It is just as popular in Kent, where there are in fact more registered herds, but there is nowhere where it looks more at home than in Petworth park, grazing with black sheep and fallow deer. The great Sussex landowners, like the Egremonts, were amongst the early enthusiasts for the breed. One of the prime movers was the same John Ellman of Glynde who developed the Southdown sheep breed.

A Sussex farmer from Firle was one of the first to send milk to London by train, but many of the Wealden smallholders with a handful of cattle and three or four wood-girt fields have had a very lean time in recent years. They cannot compete with the superb herds of prime dairy cattle, such as the Friesians of Ide Hill or the Jersey herd of Loseley Hall in the Surrey plain. Loseley, one of the great Tudor houses of Surrey, markets its products in local shops and in London, producing cream, yoghourt, ice-cream and cheeses. Many of the pedigree herds are signposted by farm gates and the importance of each breed can be judged by the frequency of its name. Friesians, Shorthorns, Jerseys, are all there. But look especially for the Red Sussex.

The vision of fat cows knee-deep in water meadows and buttercups and daisies is not entirely fake, though few of the water meadows are managed as well as they once were. The reality is often less romantic, of a struggle to find sufficient grazing without using up hay kept for winter fodder or buying in expensive feed-stuffs. July and August are amongst the wetter months but summer's high temperatures evaporate the soil moisture. The total water deficiency in the six summer months is often in excess of the equivalent of ten inches of rain and, in some recent years has exceeded that. Then the pastures are nourishment only for a hardy breed like the Red Sussex.

By the third week of the month, the lamb sales are on. 'These will grow into money, gentlemen', says the auctioneer trying to get another fiver on the bid. The lambs run distractedly round the ring on Horsmonden's playing field watched by the weathered faces of men who can tell a good half-bred lamb when they see one. There's a tweed suit with a rakish trilby, a cloth cap and a flannel shirt, the young farmers looking keen, the old looking wary. The sheep dogs sleep in the shade, giving up hope of action until the lambs, sold, stampede down the alley between the pens. The dogs wake up. The ring moves on and the next lambs arrive. Dorsets, Suffolks, Kents, Southdowns. The lorries trundle off to all parts of the country. Around the field, the apples are getting plump in the orchards, ready for auction before the month is out.

CHAPTER 8

August

Just about five miles separates the infamous summit of Gibbet Hill by the A3 trunk road in Surrey from the Great Pond of Frensham. Between them lies one of the most rugged and varied areas in the the south-east, a classic encounter with rocks, their effect on the landscape and man's response. This is the heart of the Surrey heathland. Surrey's suburban gentility creeping in stately villas and cosy cottages up the flanks of the hills, is a comparatively new aspect, scarcely more than a hundred years old, prompted by the Victorian taste for pine woodlands and wild heaths, a touch of the Scottish highlands within easy reach of the metropolis. In earlier times, the heaths were forbidding to farming and to settlement, a shunned wilderness symbolised by the gibbet that once stood on Hindhead Common and now commemorated by a stone that still lays a curse on all who try to move it.

The area was immortalised by travellers like William Cobbett, himself a Surrey man, born and bred in Farnham, as one of the most villainous spots on the earth. Like Arthur Young, he preferred the prospect of waving corn, ripe for August harvest. Now, in contrast, the barren heaths are amongst the county's main amenities, many of them being controlled by the National Trust which took possession of Gibbet Hill as far back as 1906. The Trust is now one of the main guardians of heathland landscapes with nature trails on Gibbet Hill and in the Devil's Punchbowl, a most attractive information centre on Witley Common to the north, and part control of the Country Park at Frensham. This wild landscape is developed on the rocks of the lower greensand, a series of strata that lie in the geological time-scale between the chalk to the north and the Wealden clays and sandstones. The different beds of sandstone, known as the greensands, vary a great deal as the journey from Hindhead to Frensham will show. Gibbet Hill is composed of the Hythe Beds, dry and infertile. Although there is woodland all round the car park by the A3, the walker taking the trail to the east over Gibbet Hill, following the indicator marks on the trees, is soon into open heathlands bright with the August colouring of heather and dwarf gorse.

Heath, heather, heathen. The words are all related. For the botanist the heath is an area in which heather dominates the plant community. In more general terms it was the forbidding land outside cultivation fit only for outlaws and heathens, rather like the two men who murdered a sailor on the road from Portsmouth in 1786 and had their bodies hung in chains. Hence the gibbet.

Wind-swept, ravaged by storms and fire, the heaths owe their origin not only to geology, but also to human activity. There is plentiful evidence that early man dwelt on these uplands, as hunter, iron-worker and even as cultivator. Investigation of archaeological sites has shown that open woodland, with hazel, birch and oak existed before the heather. Man cleared the land by cutting and burning. Man made the heaths, controlling the vegetational succession. In living memory, some areas were used for common grazing of livestock, bracken was cut for litter, timber and fuel was gathered. With the loss of these traditional practices, the trees are coming back to claim their territory. But there are new pressures replacing the old; walkers, riders, car parks and picnics, wearing deep tracks in the sand. Fires helped create the heaths, but when they are uncontrolled, burning in the growing season, they not only affect the vegetation, but destroy nesting sites, small mammals and insects. The authorities responsible for such areas are not just providing open spaces for visitors to enjoy, they are managers of a wide, open nature reserve, with its very special flora and fauna.

Take the heather, for example. There are three species to be found on Gibbet Hill, all in flower in August. The common ling usually dominates the drier areas with its small, pale purple flowers, sometimes shading to white. The deep purple clusters of bell heather, with tight whorls of short leaves, can turn almost red. The cross-leaved heath with pale pink clusters like small globes, prefers the wetter areas, but all three can be found in close proximity. Other heathers exist in Surrey, such as the Irish heath, but usually in cultivated gardens. Heathers take about twenty years to reach maturity and the intense fires that have ravaged the heaths periodic-ally, especially in the extremely dry summers of recent years, affect the heather adversely, giving the advantage to its competitors such as bracken and the coarse grasses such as molinia, the purple moor grass. In many areas burnt in the early summer of 1976, such as Chobham and Thursley, grasses were growing strongly within a month and new fronds of bracken unfolding. Burnt birches were sending up new shoots from the base with unusually large leaves, but the heather was reduced to a black powder. Yet, on a patch of Hindhead Common burnt in 1970, a mat of ling had re-established itself within five years, together with young seedlings of pine, birch and oak and a lovely flurry of dwarf gorse. The main flowering of the larger gorse bushes is over by August, but the brilliance of the younger shoots is a compensation. In that same burnt area is a parasitic plant known as the Common Dodder, its red thread-like stems giving it the local name of the Devil's guts. Its sweet-smelling flowers are easily overlooked, being similar at first sight to the heather itself.

Equally prolific on Gibbet Hill is the bilberry, its purple berries ripening in the late summer. Its local name, hurt, is recalled in Hurt Hill, a viewpoint half a mile to the east of Gibbet Hill. The same word appears to the north in Hurtwood, but bilberry seems to be less general than it was, being invaded by bracken. The view from either Hurt Hill or Gibbet Hill shows the difference between sandstone and clay in their effect on topography. Below are the richly cultivated lowlands of the Wealden clay. Springs break out at the junction of the two rock types, feeding the upper tributaries of the river Arun. Richer in minerals, well watered, the clays produce a typical patchwork of pasture, ploughland and woodland with medieval 'folds' like Chiddingfold, Alfold and Dunsfold nestling in the fertile land.

The settlement around Hindhead is much more recent, building sites having been taken from the commons in the nineteenth century. Infertile as it is, the sandstone provides the summits and the viewpoints. At 273 m., Gibbet Hill is the second highest summit in Surrey, the highest, Leith Hill, being in view of the wooded ridge to the north east. Another outstanding point, seen to the south, is Blackdown, the highest point in Sussex, the sandstone here producing at 280 m. a height that the chalk cannot rival in the whole of the South Downs. In clearings and rides other plants have adapted to the sterile soils, tormentil and heath bedstraw, yarrow and knapweed, ragworts and hardier members of the dandelion family such as the lesser hawkbit and chondrilla. The black knapweed needs a second look for there is another typical heathland plant, the sawwort, that resembles it closely.

Although the main gorse may be out of bloom, its seed-pod popping in the heat, the dwarf gorse is in full bloom, attracting insects like the white-tailed bumble bee. Gorse, like many other plants, once had many uses, for making dyes and wines. With heather, it was used for cheap thatching. It could be bruised to make it more palatable to animals. You may still come across a bush grazed into a natural topiary effect, probably by wild deer. An unusual member of the same family is the petty whin, hiding beneath the main heathland plants, much less spiky with small oval leaves. By August it has developed long seed pods, often attacked by weevils.

The most characteristic sound of the summer heath is the dry click-click of the stonechat, like two stones knocking together. The sound may be dull but the bird is a beauty. Conspicuous in its colouring, with black head, white neck patch and red breast, the male seems to shun cover, taking a short dipping flight from bush to bush, resting on gorse top or birch bough to utter his chatty warning. He often circles the intruder, uttering constant cries at each calling post, with the female, less colourful, doing likewise on the other side of the circuit. It may be due to my limited observation, but I have never seen a female stonechat perch higher than the male. I have watched them on the burnt stubs of gorse within yards of a main road less than a week after a severe heath fire, but the stonechat is one of many birds which suffers from a diminution of its nesting areas. Both the Dartford warbler and the wood lark are declining in breeding pairs. The Dartford warbler suffered a severe setback in the winter of 1962–63 and the summer of 1976 was nearly as disastrous. Keeping to cover, it is much less easily seen than other heathland birds.

Birds of prey such as the buzzard and the hobby use the heaths as feeding grounds, the comparatively open nature of the country giving less cover to the small birds and mammals which are their prey. But we may never see the blackcock again on its 'leks'. It was last seen at Hindhead in the 1890s, but now we have to travel to northern moorlands to witness its fabulous courting display.

Although most of the traditional deciduous trees are present at Hindhead, the skyline always seems to be dominated by the lop-sided silhouette of the Scots pine. Its seeds find a ready bed in the loose sand, although it suffers losses due to the squirrels which nibble hundreds of the green cones and strew the summer paths with the debris. The pine cone is the symbol of the Surrey Naturalists' Trust with good reason, for it ousts the oak from its pre-eminence. In Surrey, according to forestry statistics, the pine takes first place, the oak second. The pine is a native of the region gaining an early foothold after the waning of the ice sheets, but most of the pine woods are comparatively recent in origin, their planting being stimulated after the restoration of Charles II. General Monk brought pines with him from Scotland which were planted in Greenwich Park and, at the same time, John Evelyn was commending the trees for their combination of beauty and utility and actively propogating them on his Surrey estates. The popularity of the Scotch fir, as it was often known, reached its climax in the Victorian period when it added yet another touch of the Highlands to the tamer Wealden countryside.

The Scots pine is much favoured by the Forestry Commission as it regenerates easily, grows quickly and finds a ready market in the softwoods industry. Clumps of Scots pine with bushy tops on prominent hill-tops, as on Ashdown Forest, are a distinctive sight with a characteristic curl on the uppermost section of their red trunks. In serried ranks more favoured by foresters, they achieve a straighter growth but create a rather dull forest floor. Yet the pine woods are no desert for naturalists for the tree is host to nearly one hundred insects, more than the beech or the ash.

An hour's walk on Gibbet Hill illustrates nearly all the main features of heathland, its succession from open heathland to pine and oak woodland and all the problems of modern overuse. Heathland gets really exciting when there is some water about, in wet ghylls or boggy hollows. Drop down from the summit of Gibbet Hill northwards into the deep combe of the Devil's Punchbowl and the flora changes from dry, open heathland to damp deciduous woodland with oak, beech, whitebeam and hazel. Springs breaking out in abundance from the Atherfield clay at the bottom of the valley have sapped away at the sandy hillsides, undermining them and thereby creating this unusual bowl shape. In places the ground is boggy enough to hold wet patches of sphagnum moss and clumps of watermint. The nettles, wood sage, wood sorrel and willowherbs grow tall and add to the richness of the flora which includes woundworts, lesser stitchwort and ferns. A favourite haunt for feral deer, especially the roe, it comes to life in the early and late hours of the day, though I watched a green woodpecker at work at midday within a few yards of a busy public footpath.

Paths wind north beyond the marked nature trail from Highcombe Bottom towards Punchbowl Farm. The valley stream which feeds eventually into the river Wey, cuts through another rock strata called the Bargate Beds. Suddenly the wilderness gives way to a strip of rich farmland with dairy pastures and fruit, thanks to the richer nutrients of the rock with shelly limestones mixed up with the sandstone. There the wayside flowers and weeds of cultivation find a suitable foothold, but the zone is scarcely a mile wide before the tough, resistant sandstones of the Folkestone and Sandgate Beds rise up into a heathland even more dramatic than Gibbet Hill. Here you must make a choice of routes, north-west along the lanes to Churt Common and the Devil's Jumps or north-east to Thursley Common and Witley. But, as we are in Devil's territory, we must not miss his Jumps.

The path from the inn, bearing the portrait of Lloyd George, rises steeply through loose, dark brown sand to a sharp ridge capped with a rock layer so dark in colour, so distorted in structure that it looks like lumps of flaky chocolate. This is the toughest sandstone of them all, the carstone, compacted and stained with iron. It has protected the ridge from erosion, leaving three conical hills, the Devil's Jumps, one of the few viewpoints which has hardly a building in sight for mile after mile. Behind is a landscape dominated by trees. To the north, the ground falls away to a flat sandy plain, much of it owned by the National Trust, with clearly marked tracks criss-crossing the heaths toward the Great Pond at Frensham.

The Great and Little Ponds, created by the monks of Waverley Abbey as medieval fish ponds, are now the centre-pieces of a Country Park set up in 1971. The margins of the ponds are so popular, so trodden, that they are reminiscent of a coastal beach. Car access is limited by ditches and fences, but horse riders create ribbons of desert, the hoofs breaking through the grassy skin of the earth, causing rapid gullying.

Frensham is as much a nature reserve as playground. Sand lizards, natterjack toads and smooth snakes are to be found there, but are declining in numbers. Scots pine covers about 140 of the 780 acres, by far the dominant tree. The excellent handbook produced by the Hambledon Rural District Council talks of the trees as a 'fascinating study of the rise and fall of a woodland empire'. The familiar pattern is seen of pine and birch invading the heath until the oaks are established and outgrow them by their longevity. But the oak and the beech need help to regenerate and the prolific pines give a useful financial return. The damper zones where alder and willow take over are of special interest giving food and cover to a variety of birds. Alder buckthorn, essential to the life-cycle of the brimstone butterfly, grows along the wet channels.

Thursley is a nature reserve, accessible by footpath from the village of the same name and from the A3 trunk road, which runs to the east of the common. A heather-dominated area, it has been so ravaged by fire that it is the subject of a detailed annual study by the Surrey Naturalists' Trust to note the recovery or otherwise of its flora and fauna. The east side of the reserve at Warren Mere, has restricted access. A series of hammer-ponds, relics of the iron industry, attract wildfowl and fish. The bank sides and the joining channels give a suitable habitat for fenland plants. Together with the woodlands surrounding the ponds, this is a varied area rich in wildlife.

Thursley is for the specialist. For the general public, by far the best site is Witley Common, only another two miles along the A3. Here the National Trust has set up a modern, well-equipped information centre, together with a series of nature trails. The common is largely under woodland cover but the limited areas of open heath are maintained by mowing and 'swiping' with machines like giant flails to keep down the coarser vegetation, the ever-encroaching bracken and birch, and encourage the more delicate flora. Some of the plants are more readily associated with chalk soils and this is due to the sort of historic accident that makes the south-east so interesting. Materials were brought in to build up a parade ground for troops camped on the common during the last war and those materials have added a new dimension to the local soils. Many of the Surrey heaths are still used as army training grounds, noted on the map as 'Danger Areas'. The very lack of public access, the comparative lack of daily disturbance, has acted as a protection for wildlife. Even more ironic, the very ravages of tracked vehicles have led, in many cases, to a revitalisation of true heathland.

For the most part, the Surrey commons where the break was cut, the heather burnt, the bilberries picked, the winter fuel gathered, the cattle grazed, have become forested. The sandstone ridge from Wonersh to Leith Hill which includes Blackheath, Farley Heath, Hurtwood Common, Winterfold, Wotton Common, Holmwood is well wooded. The names show that it was not always so. They were once the common lands of the surrounding parishes such as Albury, Shere, Ewhurst and Cranleigh. Areas of open heath, such as Black-heath and the clearing round the Roman temple foundations on Farley Heath, are scarce, offering a few floral surprises such as sand spurrey, wintergreen, wall germander and touch-me-not-balsam.

The footpaths that thread through the pinewoods of Leith Hill and Holmbury are amongst the most popular in the region. Yet, a bare mile from Holmbury St Mary to the Iron Age camp site on the summit dispels the image of a monotonous pine ridge with oak, beech, dogwood, spindle, hazel, hawthorn, whitebeam, rowan, crab apple, holly and sweet chestnut all in evidence. The monkey puzzle trees on the summit of Leith Hill are an indication of the extensive replanting of both native and exotic trees that went on in the nineteenth century. Seeds of the monkey puzzle were only intro-duced from Chile in 1795 and tended at Kew. The history of the forest landscape is as complex as any part of the countryside. When Iron Age man was dwelling on Holmbury Hill and Anstiebury the vegetation was probably cleared, resembling the heaths of Thursley.

The highest point of Leith Hill is a tantalising 294 m which induced John Hull to erect an observation tower to achieve a nice, round one thousand feet (305 m). The view from the top is un-impeded, witnessing the great sweep of the sandstone ridge back to Hascombe and Hindhead, and finally to Blackdown.

Blackdown is another isolated hill with views south, east and west. The 500 acres of its summit are yet another possession of the National Trust. They have a special interest as a favourite perambulation of Alfred Lord Tennyson who spent his last years in Aldworth House. The circuit of the paths is less than one mile, yet it sums up the same vegetative competition we have seen on other heaths. Detailed studies of the area have shown the same shrinkage of true heath, the same success of bracken. Bracken dominates by its height and shade, killing off its competitors. The multitude of small spores under each fern so prominent in August show its capacity for further seeding. But bracken is less successful in exposed sites where cold winds blow inhibiting its growth above the surrounding plants. So the heather finds its own unrivalled territory on the west side of the hill.

On Blackdown, as elsewhere, the wood ants stream along their private highways, cutting purposefully across paths, mountaineering up pine barks, ascending oak trees, smothering the acorns, gathering pine needles and the debris of the forest into ant hills 1 m or more high. Disturb them at your peril. The thin injections of formic acid can be as sharp as a bite. Many seeds are dispersed by ants in their eternal labour and thereby helped to colonise the empty spaces. Some aphids, abundant in dry summers, are farmed by the ants for their honey dew. The larvae of the silver-studded blue, a common butterfly of the Surrey heathlands, are used similarly as a kind of milking parlour.

Apart from Blackdown, heathland is generally less prominent in Sussex, but rewarding patches are found throughout the narrow outcrop of greensand which forms a long range of hills below the South Downs. Woolbeding, Iping and Ambersham are typical. Ambersham is one of the many surprises that Sussex holds in its gentle folds. Coming off the Heyshott Downs past chalk quarries rich with summer flora down through the straggly green that cuts right through the centre of the village of Heyshott, you expect the landscape to change to high farming, but instead you are confronted with Ambersham Common, a deep, heather-filled bowl looking like a lost outpost of the Scottish highlands. Showing all the features common to other heathlands, Ambersham has some riddles of its own, such as a capping of broken flints on its 60 m summit. How the flints got there, on top of sandstone strata, so far from their place of origin is best left to the speculation of geologists. Perhaps they were washed there by an ancient incursion of the sea breaking through the chalk, flint-laden Downs.

One of the largest and one of the most closely studied commons left in Sussex is in the heart of the county at Chailey, a name derived from 'gorse field'. Its prominent windmill reputedly stands at the exact centre of the county. The common survived the nineteenth-century enclosure movement to become a major amenity in the area. Controlled by a committee composed of the local authorities, the Sussex Naturalists' Trust and the Chailey Common Society set up in 1962, its flora and fauna have been recorded annually. More than 269 flowering species and sub-species on record are a tribute not only to the observers but to the variation of the common from dry, open heath to areas of fen. In the boggy areas, carefully screened from the public areas, are such rarities as bog asphodel, marsh gentian, marsh fragrant orchid and the associated bog bush cricket. There are wet zones in the public sector where a small stream cuts south from the road then runs right across the place, but the nature trail has been laid out north-east of the windmill on the higher ground.

In a typical year, about 72 different species of bird have been sighted, 46 of them breeding on the common. Stonechats are always in evidence, about 6 pairs being resident. But the greatest numbers of breeding pairs are of willow warblers, 86 pairs. Robins, blackbirds, house martins and wrens are all in excess of 50 breeding pairs, with linnets, meadow pipits, dunnocks, blue tits and great tits close behind. The smaller mammals of the common have been recorded in an unusual but harmless way, by trapping them in empty bottles. The results revealed 47 common shrews, 4 pigmy shrews, 4 water shrews, 20 bank voles, 7 field voles, 7 wood mice and 1 yellow-necked mouse. No less than 7 small mammals were found together in one bottle!

On the southern perimeter of the common is one small cottage where the owner is old and wise enough to recall the days when the common had its traditional uses. He still cuts a little heather himself to make tiny thatched roofs on bird nesting boxes that surround his front gate. His affection for the birds is nearly as great as his love of the common and its history. His only complaint is the summer drought on the sandstone that makes gardening a heart-breaking chore.

The first day of the month is Lammastide, once celebrated by eating a loaf made from the first cut of wheat. On that day, too, the hay fields became common grazing until the spring. The lammas lands, or half-year lands, were amongst the common fields lost to parliamentary enclosure in the first decades of the nineteenth century. Imperial in its name, imperious in its heat, August is the crown of the year. Recent dry hot summers have brought the cereal harvest forward to July, yet a wet season in the same decade has seen a poor harvest being dragged from sodden fields well into October. August remains the hub of harvest with sparrows and linnets invading the heavy drying corn heads for a first plunder before the combines crunch in. Then the rooks and starlings and pigeons descend for the gleaning and the hares hop out at dusk with their ears pricking out above the short stubble. Young pheasants and partridge whisper in the cut corn.

The modern harvester sits like a pilot over his controls, ears baffled against the roar, mouth covered against the dust, while lorries buzz to and fro like satellites to collect the precious ears. Barley is now the major crop in the region covering nearly one-third of the total cropland, nearly half in West and East Sussex where the downland plateau has become as much part of the arable scene as the lower chalk platform that fronts both the North and South Downs. Wherever there is a fairly level surface of chalk, there are the big modern arable fields; the slopes of the Hog's Back, the East Kent plateau, the Isle of Thanet, the tops of the Downs. Big fields with scarcely a hedge in sight to interrupt the march of the new armoured brigade. Many of the largest fields occupy the sites of the early open medieval fields and retain the visual impact those common arable fields must have had. The large fields on the South Downs have replaced the open grasslands.

There has been less change in the field patchwork of the Weald which is such a feature of the views from Gibbet Hill and Leith Hill, but elsewhere there has been extensive removal of hedgerows to make the small intakes and closes more suitable to modern farming. There are parts of the North Downs which in ten years have changed dramatically with the extension of cereal acreage, some fields being up to a mile wide. Behind the harvester, the straw is chopped into neat bales, but even that is changing in favour of the huge rolls of straw slumped around the edge of fields, a favourite haven for sheep in windy weather. Quicker to make and fairly impervious to weather, the half-ton bundles stand ready to be rolled out for winter feed.

William Cobbett said he had never seen better cornfields than those on the Goodwood Estate in West Sussex. He would not be disappointed now. The flat plains on the fertile gravelly soils between the Downs and the coast are one of the bread-baskets of the region. Halnaker Mill, built in 1756 to grind corn for the poor of the parish, stands amongst the cut harvest, its sails as useless as broken wings, recalling the days of horse and oxen, of scythe and flail. Its setting is only surpassed by Chillenden Mill, an old post mill high above the broad acres of the East Kent plateau. The redundant tools of old harvests are not quite forgotten, some of them being gathered in local museums, such as the pioneering open air museum of Weald and Downland Life at Singleton, just to the north of Goodwood.

CHAPTER 9

September

Beachy Head in mid-September holds on to its holiday image. The buses roll up from Eastbourne, the car parks are still busy and people bring out their folding chairs to enjoy the cliff-top breezes and the last of the summer sun as it approaches the equinox. The sun may still bounce with brilliance from the white cliffs, dazzling the sea. The lighthouse, focus for all attention, stands proudly in the teeth of the surging waters nibbling at the rock face. Above the murmurs of the waves, there is the familiar cry of herring gulls and jackdaws, the less familiar thin sound of the rock pipit and, with luck, the short guttural ag-ag-ag of the fulmar. On the cliff face there is a flourish of colour with wild carrot, wild parsnip and sea beet, all with thick fleshy leaves able to withstand blown salt spray. The cliffs form a special rock garden, out of reach of interference from man, with rock sea lavender, rock samphire, red valerian, sea bindweed hanging on to every patch of soil held in the rocky joints and ledges.

On the short springy turf above, the plants have a two-fold adaptation. The coastal winds and the incessant tread of people give the plants their special features. They keep their heads well down. You can almost map the favoured paths of passers-by by the size and frequency of flowers. Apart from the viper's bugloss hanging on to the cliff's edge, the only flower that dares the immediate environs of the view over the lighthouse is the common daisy, and, occasionally, the dwarf thistle, small, tufty purple head squatting within its broad rosette of spiky leaves creating a halo of dampness beneath its foliage even in the driest summers. Downslope towards the Birling Gap, the flowers reassert themselves, grow taller, in their last splendid affirmation of the growing season. Marjoram, wild basil and thyme, centaury and autumn gentian thrust up even through bare chalk, milkwort and eyebright, harebell and clustered bell-flower and another remarkable member of the thistle family, the carline thistle, the yellow bracts so pale that they often look dead, especially as the dead heads stand throughout the winter. Found with the scabious and often doomed to be overlooked because of its resemblance to them is the pride of Sussex, the round-headed rampion. The dark purple upturned petals forming a small globular head seem to get rarer every year though the flower is still abundant in some localities on the South Downs.

Inland from the grassy walk along the cliff top, the scrubland of privet and hawthorn is swept by the sea winds into grotesque shapes, the branches twisting away from the bent trunks to the leeward side. Salt spray from winter gales burns the leaves of trees more than a mile away. Now, in late summer, the bushes are rustling with yellowhammers, chaffinches, linnets and whitethroats. This is the setting for one of the year's greatest dramas. Amongst the to-ing and fro-ing of small birds you suddenly become aware of a pattern of movement. A high twittering fills the air. An army of small black and white dots invades the clear sky, advancing steadily from the east towards the headland. The air becomes filled with swallows and martins, as many as a thousand passing each hour. Other flocks come from inland, following well-defined routes, all gathering above the highest point of the cliffs, wheeling, circling, screaming. The migration is on. Some birds have gone already, the swifts and some of the martins. Some will stay until November, but September is the time of mass movement. The birds often move back from the coast for a few miles, feeding along the rivers and on the Downs, moving back rhythmically to the coasts as if gathering strength before the inner sense triggers them off, launching them on the immense journey to the far south across the equator. At Dungeness more than 5,000 swallows have been sighted in one day, the September total for that one migration point being 50,000 swallows, 14,000 house martins and 17,000 sand martins. In the same month more than 2,000 meadow pipits have departed.

The whole length of the south coast becomes a sort of giant airport lounge of the avian world with musterings for departure and arrivals and a general air of restlessness. Many of the warblers, tree pipits, flycatchers, redstarts and wheatears rest for a few days on the shingle ridges of Dungeness. Siskins, reed buntings, dunnocks and bearded tits increase in numbers. Redstarts from Dungeness have been tracked by ringing to Morocco, whitethroats from Sandwich Bay have been found in the Lebanon and North Italy, meadow pipits in Spain, spotted flycatchers in Algiers, pied flycatchers in Portugal. The movement is inexorably south.

Observations along the Sussex coast give a list of September departures, fulmar, garganey, hobbies leaving their heathlands and parks, quail leaving the open downs, Kentish plover, lark, wheatear, whinchat, chiffchaff, yellow wagtail and, of course, the terns, heading for the southernmost reaches of Africa. During their last few days at Pagham Harbour, the terns seem to spend all of their time feeding, plummeting into the ebbing tide time and time again for small fish and crustaceans.

The traffic is not all one way. The arrival lounge is busy, too. Coastal birds like gadwall and widgeon, tufted duck and common scoter are coming in. Turnstones, dunlins and the first fieldfares are arriving from the north. Black-headed gulls and common gulls arrive from Russia and Northern Europe, hen harriers from Finland. Robins move in, too, swelling the home-bound numbers. Movements of some species are very complex, some leaving, some arriving, such as oyster-catchers, knots, merlins, stonechats and pied wagtails.

The impact is felt well inland. At the Kingley Vale reserve, the migrant movements have been recorded. Leaving in September are the nightingales, spotted flycatchers, turtle doves, juvenile cuckoos left to their own devices by the parent birds, and most of the warblers. Chiffchaffs, whitethroats and tree pipits may remain until October. Then the redwings and fieldfares arrive to plunder the yew berries and scatter the seeds far and wide, thereby extending the yew groves. In that same reserve, the list of resident birds makes interesting reading. By far the most abundant are robins and chaffinches, followed numerically by the wrens, dunnocks, goldcrests, coal tits, great tits and yellowhammers. Movements, national rather than international, also take place amongst some of the more common birds such as thrushes and blackbirds. The foliage of the trees and the dense evergreen of the yew groves make bird observation in places like Kingley Vale more difficult than the more open ground of the coastal reserves, but a quiet spot on the path up to Bow Hill and a pair of binoculars will bring most of the birds into view at some time or other. The kestrels are more prominent than ever. You don't need binoculars to see as many as ten kestrels hovering in line astern at eye level above the upper combe, and half a dozen magpies floating across the darkness of the opposite woodland. Even the calm of Windover Hill, alongside the Long Man of Wilmington, with a pheasant clearing its throat in a soft, damp morning, can be shattered by kestrels, rooks and magpies in combat, diving, twisting, screaming for mastery. The rooks chase the kestrels in the air. The kestrels dive at the rooks when they settle on the ground. The magpies chase everything including each other before leaving the field for a quieter copse over to the east. When the kestrels are left as the victors and take their ease towards the vale below, a mass of finches, dunnocks, linnets rises in protest and mobs them. The uproar can last for hours.

A bonus for the visitor to coastal migration areas such as Pagham, Dungeness and Sandwich Bay is the late season flora of salt marsh and shingle. The coast has a delayed rhythm, the sea gathering its warmth later than the land, retaining it longer so that summer lingers on into early autumn. The coast is more equable, cooler in high summer, warmer in deep winter. The plants adapt to their special habitat, with a zonation related to changing sea level and tidal movements. On the shingle ridges, sea holly and yellow-horned poppy, sea cabbage and sea beet grow together with more common invaders like ragwort, mayweed, sorrel, dock, deadly nightshade and even a patch of herb robert. At the tidal limit, sea aster begins to dominate with its lovely blue flower around a yellow centre, with sea spurrey, red goosefoot and sea purslane. On the wetter mudflats, glasswort forms the base cover with its obscure flowers reddening the points of its short, stubby, translucent stems. It used to be harvested to burn for soda used in the glass industry, hence its name. The ringed plover scuttles over mud banks, red-shank and greenshank dabble in the watery channels, pipits dive after thistledown, curlew and whimbril call overhead and a heron waits silently until a 90 cm eel comes within its patient reach.

The natural highways to the coasts are nearly as interesting as the more famous migration points. The Sussex river valleys cutting through the Downs are wide enough to hold a variety of countryside, meadows, small areas of fenland, harvested fields, patches of wood-land, with an appropriate diversity of flora and insect life to give rich feeding grounds for birds on the move. New canalisation and reinforcement of banks on some stretches of the Ouse and the Arun have destroyed much of the flora for a season, but on other stretches of water, especially in quiet backwaters like Amberley Wild Brooks where the Sussex Naturalists have created a small reserve, the September flora rivals the seashore. Most interesting of the plants which adapt to slow-moving, often brackish, waters are those with three-petalled flowers like the water plantain, arrowhead, frogbit and flowering rush, all flowering late in the season. Among the juncus rush, the irises and phragmites closer to the banks are rich colours of the purple and yellow loosestrifes, the former being dominant in some channels. On the steep banks and in wet patches of meadow are the tongue-twisting flora like trifid bur-marigold, touch-me-not-balsam, marsh stitchwort, water forget-me-not, celery-leaved buttercup and stinging nettles. Clumps of watermint attract more flies than any other plant and may be smothered by a second crop of tortoiseshell butterflies. On the water, amongst the plantain, is water crowfoot and the yellow water lily, its flowers turning into the familiar seed-head shaped like a brandy bottle. Amberley is a haunt of herons, seldom a September day passing without sight of a half dozen of them flying low and slow from one channel to another.

Most of these water-loving plants can be found on the channels of the water-meadows bordering the Ouse, between Lewes and Newhaven. Footpaths follow both banks of the river accessible from the narrow crossing at Southease and followed at this point by the South Downs Way. Within sight of the round-towered Norman church the warblers and reed buntings are especially abundant early in the month. They are found, too, right across the region in the drained fens between Deal and Sandwich, around the village of Worth.

One of my favourite walks follows the line of the disused Arun Canal just to the north of Amberley Wild Brooks. The canal once linked the south coast with the Thames by way of the rivers Arun and Wey. The route was never a commercial success though it bore its cargoes of timber, coal and grain. Abandoned locks and quays can be found in the middle of farmland, such as Pallingham Quay. The most accessible section of the canal is reached by footpath from Hardham Priory, now a ruin in a farm courtyard, on the main A29 south of Pulborough. The flora varies according to the amount of standing water left in the canal. At one point near Waterfield an old lock hidden by hawthorn and willow stands like an oasis especially in the period of summer drought. Cattle and horses mooch across to it constantly and birds seem to outnumber the berries on the hawthorn. Finches and tits stand on every twig while the warblers shuffle along the lower branches. Swallows and martins patrol the channel. On the meadows, lapwings flock in their hundreds and migrants gather. A scoter rises in alarm from the reed beds and Canada geese roll in to join the lapwings. Generally, the wildfowl, like the swans, prefer the open moving water of the Arun itself nearby. Close to Hardham, the canal is almost silted up in a dark tunnel of ancient willows where trees fall and refuse to die, sending up hosts of parallel branches like wands from the fallen trunk. The wrens find new boldness and emerge from their dank hiding places to sound a warning. As the wind rises, the willows rub leaning branches together and groan, increasing the sense of desolation. But this is no desert for insects and fungi.

One of the most striking plants of the water channels is the teasel, the last of its blue flowers hanging in rings round the bold head, still sought hungrily by peacock butterflies. Even when bare, its prickly head and stem are gathered for winter decoration. It once had a more important function for teasing cloth. Many are the varieties of thistles along the banksides, the creeping thistle and the spear thistle all inspected by the hordes of goldfinches in their chattering forays from the hawthorn scrub. At Hardham, the footpath crosses the road and links up with yet another unofficial nature reserve, the disused railway line that once linked Pulborough with Petersfield.

This track would make a magnificent long-distance walkway, much of it in cuttings and on embankments still untouched and unenclosed. One section bounding the north side of Ambersham Common adds to the value of that heathland. The section near Hardham cuts through a Roman camp which stood on the alignment of Stane Street. The railway cuttings give shade, shelter and isolation to flora and fauna. The tracks were often made up with materials from outside the immediate locality so that lime-loving plants may be found amongst the normal sandstone flora. In a recent dry summer I saw more flowers of the chalk country, including nettle-leaved bellflowers, on that railway line than I did on the burnt, barren downs to the south. Apart from the banquet of dewberries and blackberries, the tansy attracts with its pungent smell, the yellow flowers being even stronger to the nose than the leaves. There are enough culinary and medical herbs along that line to make a medieval apothecary happy. More than forty flowering plants in September is food enough for the senses. The canal and railway sections can be joined by a footpath from Watersfield by way of Sandy Lane to Coates and Fittleworth through woodland of especially fine oaks, part of the Barlavington Estate.

One similar section of disused railway running south-west from Henfield in mid-Sussex is used as a right-of-way from the village, making a useful link with the paths on the banks of the Adur.

The attraction of the Sussex rivers is being celebrated by a new wildfowl refuge on the wet zone between the Arun and the steep, tree-lined cliff of Arundel Park. Ponds, islands, loafing sites and enclosures for the birds, hides and information centre for the visitors are intended to encourage not only the native wildfowl but also the introduction of exotic species. A refuge for exotic wildfowl already exists in East Sussex on the lowlands of Halland, at Bentley, on a small tributary of the Ouse. Flamingos and white peacocks join with ducks and geese from all over the world, clipped and contained in fenced enclosures, to fill the Sussex air with unaccustomed sounds.

The twin features of Sussex river valleys and the coast come together in the Seven Sisters Country Park at the mouth of the Cuckmere, only two miles west of Beachy Head, though the flora of the water channels is not as rich as elswhere. One of the recent innovations at the Interpretative Centre has been the publication of a new style of nature trail, walks designed to introduce the varied barns of the area, most appropriate to a centre which is itself housed in a converted oak-framed barn of the eighteenth century. The trails take in the enormous medieval tithe barns such as Alciston, Burlow and Wilmington, where the monks gathered their tenths of the harvest and other products of their extensive estates, to the modern asbestos-covered, concrete-pillared structures of the recent decade. Many have fallen into disuse, many converted to other uses. But enough have survived agricultural depression and the mechanisation of threshing to illustrate the past centuries of harvest and an indelible part of the country scene.

The vision of the corn harvest, cut, collected and confined is never far from another cliff line that maintains an even greater diversity of flora than Beachy Head and the Seven Sisters. Since the National Trust purchased Bockhill Farm north of St Margaret's Bay, an unexcelled cliff-top walk of more than five miles from Walmer to Dover has been made possible with alternative parallel tracks inland making a suitable return journey, one of them following the old Walmer road to St Margaret's church. A diversion down to the bay at St Margaret's is essential if only for the vegetation clinging to the face of the chalk cliffs and the zonation of seaweeds on the rock platform below the south cliff. Two deep, parallel grooves through the flint-surfaced chalk mark an old routeway used only at low tide. The tide here hurries in with great speed and traps a regular quota of holiday-makers round the headland. The usual chalk flora is augmented by extensive scrubland and by the Pines Garden, only created from derelict land in 1970 and already a dramatic proof of what can be achieved in a short time, though much of the achievement is in the form of exotica not native to the chalk, ornamental shrubs, dwarf conifers and flowering trees being the main features. The arable fields of Bockhill approach close to the cliff edge leaving a wide strip of grassland as a walk way. Farmland, grassland, scrub, cliff and foreshore create the diversity for yet another port of call for migrant birds.

In times past, and not so very long ago at that, September was marked by a human migration too, when thousands of Londoners left the summer-stifled city to work in the hopfields and apple orchards of Kent. Their temporary 'homes' are an odd feature of rural architecture, rows of spartan brick and corrugated iron huts hiding behind hedgerows. Most of them are empty now, but one or two still sport a washing line, a pram and other signs of the nomadic life. It is a far cry from the traditional scene when one farm alone, with more than 1,000 acres would face an annual migration of more than 40,000 people seeking their annual breath of fresh air, for many their only holiday and the chance to earn enough money to buy winter clothing for the family. The Falstaffian humour, the hard work combined with an air of festival, have often been recorded. The real celebrities were the 'scratchers', the experienced women pickers who would be first into the hop gardens at seven in the morning and scratch away at the green cones with practised speed until the sun rose enough to dispel the morning dew. By picking when the hops were wet they filled their bushels at twice the speed of the average picker. The early bird really caught the worm then. The farmer could object to 'dirty picking' if too many leaves went in with the fruit, but there was little he could do about moisture content. Hop picking in the days of hand labour could go on into the early days of November, with fires in the fields to keep the worst of the cold and damp out. The festival was no fun in a wet autumn and the tiny huts lost their holiday camp atmosphere to become more like bleak barracks. Pickers were paid by a system of tokens, made of metal or wood, or even paper. These tokens, reputedly introduced by Toke of Godinton in 1767, are found in many local museums such as Maidstone, Battle and Lewes.

The farmer rubs the hop in his hand until the yellow pollen clustered by the stem stains his hands. If the stem comes away cleanly then the crop may be ready for picking. The narrow tractors chug along the rows of bines, each bine cut with a scythe, then dragged unceremoniously through the upper hooks so that the hops lie all one way across the cart behind the tractor. The pickers, dressed in yellow oilskins, work two or three to a tractor. The load is then shuttled to the sorting shed where the bines are hung up on a moving rack. The leaves are picked off and blown out of the shed on to rotting, steaming piles, sometimes used as a manure. Some hand labour is still needed to sort any remaining leaves from the hops which are then taken to the oast house for drying. It's all over by the end of the month. A pile of shoddy and old rags waits in one corner of the courtyard to be led out on to the fields, for hops are a hungry crop and the soil needs a lot of fertiliser.

The traditional oast house, usually round in shape with a conical wooden cap that swung to the wind, such a characteristic feature of the Kent countryside, is also found in Sussex and more rarely in

Surrey. In the heyday of hops in the nineteenth century the crop was a favourite for the small farmer, some of the gardens being as small as half an acre, but more usually between three and ten acres. The small, free-standing oast was introduced in the early years of that century, the square type coming into use much later. Three or four oasts in a cluster, each needing about thirty acres to keep them fully used, were the symbols of richer farmers or landowners. Many of the single oasts have found a new use now as much-sought-after houses and 'cottages', but many of the larger groups are still in use though new style drying plants have been built.

Hop-growing is much older than the oast house. Hops grow wild in hedgerows throughout the south-east, but one area that lays an apocryphal claim to the first commercial crops in Tudor England is the Stour valley east of Canterbury where oasts still abound. There a farm called Hoplands is close by a village called West Bere, a happy conjunction. The word 'oast' seems to have Flemish origins, yet another instance of the impact of immigrant people on the countryside of the region. Map all the oast houses in the region and you have a picture of hop-growing at its greatest extent. But hops were always a risky crop, a gamble even. Expensive to grow, they depended on good harvests. A few poor seasons with strong winds and heavy rain, together with a change in government excise policies, could lead to ruin for the smaller grower. Hops are still grown in 129 Kent parishes, but the centre of the activity is the mid-Kent area, especially around Yalding and Paddock Wood. It was at Beltring near Paddock Wood that I saw the hand-pickers at work in the late 1960s. The very next year the machines moved in and the gardens roared to a very different sound.

With the entry to the Common Market, change is going on all the time. Classic names like the 'Fuggle hop of Horsmonden' or the 'Golding of Malling' give way to the 'Wye Challenger' and the 'Wye Northdown' and 'Target'. New seedless varieties are being introduced at Little Chart which, ironically, claims to have the oldest hop-garden in the country. To produce a new pure strain every other male hop, including the wild ones, has to be eradicated. The same principle applied to the most unusual strawberry field I have ever seen, in the sandy soils of Sandwich Bay, producing plants, not fruits. The plants were for export only as top-grade. Their location was entirely due to their isolation from other strawberry fields. New species of hop, new types of wiring, a new powdered hop factory at Rainham; the countryside reflects the changing economics of farming.

An unusual effect of hops on the countryside is seen in the unusually tall hedges that surround the hop-gardens. Often nearly 4.6 m high, they are dominated by hawthorn, suggesting that they were planted in the last century. But other hedges have a strong component of hazel, with dogwood, oak, holly and other plants present. Kent farmers were already famous for their hedgerows in the late eighteenth century and it is likely that many of the hedge-rows with three or four species date from the introduction of hops in Tudor times.

These tall hop windbreaks have escaped the burning that has ravaged so many field boundaries as a result of stubble burning following the grain harvest. The creeping flames have become almost a ritual celebration of the end of summer, an unwelcome one in terms of the damage it does to hedgerows and trees and the animals and birds which use them as shelter and highway. Hedge-row trees used to supply one-third of the timber of the south-east and medieval laws protected the saplings. Neither the burning nor the new mechanised hedge-trimmers have any such power of selection. Whenever I see the monsters grunting along the lanes, I think of the shepherd on Shirley Moor who still trims the hedges himself with an eye to their botanical richness.

After the hop picking, the apples are ready. 'Beauty of Bath' and 'Worcester Pearmains' have already started on their way to market, but the real Kentish favourites, the 'Cox's Orange pippins' and 'Bramley seedlings' are both late pickers. October rather than September is the climax of the main crop, though there will be a fair number of windfalls by then. Bramleys occupy a greater acreage than any other apple in the south-east, the big green cookers having maintained their popularity since they were introduced early in the nineteenth century. They are finding favour on the Continent, too. Second in acreage is the 'Cox's', a lovely crisp eating apple that tastes as good as it looks. Perfected by Richard Cox, a retired brewer in the 1830s, it is another apple that has stood the test of time.

In the older orchards, the special wide-bottomed ladders rest against the trees; boxes smelling of fresh pine wait by the barns. In the newer orchards, the trees are smaller, bush-like, easier to reach and often bearing a greater quota of fruit to foliage, and it's the fruit that matters. Some farmers are experimenting with the pyramid system, the branches trained along wires. New styles for old apples. There are new types of apple, too, 'Golden Delicious' in their trim green ranks, 'Ida Reds' hanging in dark red clusters, the perfect Christmas apple. September in the fruit areas looks as opulent as a Palmer water colour. There is more science than romance in the orchards around the East Malling Research Centre. A right-of-way from the church at East Malling village leads eastwards through the strictest landscape of experimental plots to the outskirts of Maidstone.

Some of the windfall apples may be lifted for cider; many will still be on the ground when the sheep and pigs are brought in to graze. Some apples will be doomed to rot unwanted, dumped into ditches because of the strange economics of fruit farming, the cost of picking, storing and transport being greater than the return to the farmer. The farm-gate sale gets more popular every year, many farmers selling their entire crop in this way. The bulk of the fruit is taken by lorries to the new packing and refrigerator plants that have sprung up in the bigger villages, monster plants quite out of scale with the earlier domestic and industrial architecture. Time, no doubt, will make them as acceptable as the oast house, but their materials and styles are a major break from the local vernacular traditions that have made the garden of England settlements as visually pleasing as its orchards.

CHAPTER 10

October

The hop bines are draped round the church door and over the font. Apples line the aisles in rosy rows. Garden produce nestles greenly by the steps of the nave and the pulpit. The harvest festival greets the first days of October. All is safely gathered in. But not quite. 'Cox's' and 'Bramleys' still hang in the orchards like glowing memories of summer gone. Conference and Comice pears are still swelling to perfection before the frosts and gales of autumn ravage the countryside. There are other harvests yet to come.

One of the panels in the beaten lead font at Brooklands Church in Romney Marsh depicts October, but the worn and scarcely legible legend closely resembles the word 'viticole', the month of the vines. The image shows a man treading grapes in a tub. The grape harvest, once widespread in the Norman south, has had a resurrection in recent years helped by long hot summers blessed with Mediterranean warmth. There are fields in the south-east where it is known that hops and orchards replaced vineyards in the past. Now farmers can show you fields where orchards have been grubbed up for new vines. So far the scale is small, the largest vineyard near Battle being about twenty acres in extent and most of them considerably less, two or three acres, the size of a football field. Most of the grapes are of the 'Mueller-Thurgau' variety, developed from 'Sylvaner' and 'Riesling' stock. Harvested in October, they produce wines reminiscent of the Moselle region. Growing near the northern limit of vines, they make up in quality what they lack in quantity, wines for the connoisseur never likely to oust the hop and barley from popular affection. The industry has moved far beyond the enthusiastic amateur with a vinestock growing into his greenhouse, though there are many of those happy initiators in the south-east. Southern vineyards are now an established commercial proposition with their produce on sale in London stores, on ocean-going liners and even for export to Paris. Centre of the trade is Horam in Sussex where just the right combination of deep soils and sun-catching slopes occurs. Outside the company showrooms, ironically, is an old cider press, tribute to another beverage that has almost ceased to be brewed in the area. Vinestocks can be bought at Newick in Sussex and winetasting is a regular feature at Chilgrove in the same county. Six acres of vines spread up the lower slopes of the forested ridge at Hascombe in Surrey, the county which can also boast a research centre at Ockley, on the Roman road to London. Did the Romans introduce vines a thousand years before the Normans? Several small vineyards have been established in the Kent fruit areas, three acres at Nettlestead, ten acres at Biddenden, others at Little Chart and Penshurst. The number grows each year.

Chart Sutton on the ragstone ridge south of Maidstone is one of the three places in Kent where vines were recorded in the Domesday survey. There is a fertile, south-facing escarpment, crossed by a Roman road, that seems to be dreaming of vines in the summer sun. But this slope is the centre not of vines but of another October harvest which is special to the area, the Kentish cob. Old cob plantations of nutteries are found in many famous gardens such as Sissinghurst, but most of the commercial plantations are found on the one ridge south of Maidstone. There are only about 700 acres left, mostly of the filbert variety introduced by Mr Lambert of

Goudhurst in the nineteenth century. The diminishing acreage of this crop is surprising because prime cobs fetch a good price and they seem to be the perfect crop, needing little attention, give an abundant harvest every year and fall easily to the ground when the tree is shaken, whether by man or wind. They harvest late and store easily, fitting nicely into the fruit farmer's annual rhythm.

The cob seems the answer to the lazy man's dream, a bountiful return for minimum effort. But farming is never as easy as that. Rooks can break the nuts in half. Squirrels pilfer a small proportion and even tits will jam a nut into the 'sprod' or fork of a tree and prize the nut from its tough, protective case. The picking needs to be timed to perfection, just before the main leaf falls, otherwise the gathering is made more difficult. Weeds and aphids need the usual chemical treatments. Yet eighty pounds of nuts gathered in an hour is a genial reward. Mature trees will yield about fifty pounds of nuts, about two tonnes an acre. A new tree may not yield for twenty years, but new 'wands' can be grafted on to old stubs to give a quicker return. The cob has its own vocabulary like 'wanding', cutting the new shoots, and 'brutting' for cutting the side shoots, each process having its own special tool. A brand new plantation near Ightham shows that the cob is not yet out of favour.

There is a public footpath right along the crest of the ragstone ridge from Ulcombe westwards to the Suttons, Boughton Monchelsea and Linton that traverses orchards and cobs and small fruits and a succession of splendid country 'seats', but one of the best areas for a short, circular walk taking in the pleasures of late harvest is around Plaxtol, a Saxon name with the meaning of playground. The name appears in various guises in the south-east, such as Plaistow, but at Plaxtol, on the same wooded ridge west of the Medway valley, the name is especially felicitous. From the National Trust beech clump at Gover Hill on the edge of Mereworth Woods, an old, deeply worn track leads down from oak wood and chestnut coppice past oast houses to cross the willow-lined stream towards the village. Only a half-mile to the north, on a side road, is the stone-built manor house of Old Soar, a remarkable survivor from the thirteenth century, occasionally open to the public. Most of the cob plantations lie to the north of the village along the footpath to Basted which links up with a choice of leafy lane or a longer trackway up the western slopes of the valley back to Mereworth Woods. Oast, cottage and barn find a ready market for conversion to modern residences, for this gentlest of playgrounds is within easy reach of London.

Another fruitful area, in every sense of the word, is the Medway valley from Maidstone to Yalding. The riverside walk is punctuated by the fascination of lock gates of the old Medway Navigation and as rich a collection of medieval bridges as any river can boast in such a short journey. Swans break the reflection of oast houses on the banks and disturb the concentration of anglers crouched under their green umbrellas, lost in their private interpretations of wind drag and water currents. The fishermen's notebooks reveal an eccentric view of the countryside, mirror carps lured with small potatoes, doublers tempted with cheese and brown bread. Every man has his own secret of success, baits hidden in little boxes. Every year the gear and tackle becomes more sophisticated and even the little boys have the professional trappings of keep-nets draped in the water to secure their scarce prizes, fibre-glass rods and collapsible chairs. So involved are the fishermen in their watery contest that they seem indifferent to the wheeling congregation of martins that often fills the air above them, a rallying point for hundreds of birds before the late migration.

A new 'cob' has arrived on the scene in recent years. The rage for hops in the nineteenth century has been equalled by the interest in maize which can be found growing on every soil in the region, from the fertile alluvium of Romney Marsh to the thin, sandy soils of the Surrey heaths, even on the very doors of London at Orpington. The tall plants grown mostly for green fodder have had such success that the cobs with their distinctive colourful tassels have filled out well enough to prove a great attraction at the farm gate sales. In times when livestock feed is so expensive, the sheer quantity of high-grade fodder that maize produces is of increasing importance.

The old cob, the tree crop, was developed from the native hazel tree which grows widely in the region. The hazel is found in association with oak woodland and is a main constituent of many hedge-rows. Pollen analysis on archaeological sites has shown that the hazel was once even more widespread, even dominant at times, in the Bronze Age. We can visualise the use of the nuts for food, the wands and pliable branches for making simple huts and stores and fences. Hazel wands are still part of the October building scene with the thatcher at work, using them to keep bundles of straw in place in a newly thatched roof. Thatching survives as a local art and there are farmers at Faversham and Bethersden who harvest their cereals with the old corn binder so as to leave long straw to sell to the thatchers. The thatcher at work is one of the brightest vignettes of the October countryside. I saw one recently near Sittingbourne sitting astride the roof ridge of an unpretentious brick cottage which was wearing its fresh straw like a new bonnet. Ears of corn were still hanging from some of the long wheaten straws. In the thatcher's hand was a fearsome looking tool, a 120 cm-long knife with an ash handle used for trimming the straw to the right length. Known as an eaves knife, it looked more like a sword with a deep groove down one side of the blade. The inscription engraved on it was undecipherable, but the thatcher knew it had been in his family for more than two hundred years. His face, warm with sweat and the morning sun, reflected the content of the craftsman, for that roof was as artistic as it was functional. The owner of the cottage was much less relaxed for he had known eaves knives to cut through electricity cables and telephone wires just as easily as through straw. But he was proud of his new decorative roof, fashioned from the simplest materials. Rumour has it that an imitation thatch made of plastic is being used elsewhere in the region, but we did not pursue that topic of conversation.

He was lucky to have such fine weather for the roof work for October is, on average, the wettest month of the year and can turn the baked ground of late summer into a quagmire. The earth is ready for seed fall. Still, there are days so quiet that you can hear the plop of apples and acorns falling, then the winds come roaring up the Channel and turn the woodlands into a deluge of twigs and small branches. The little boys don't wait for the wind to shake the horse chestnut trees. For the pensive walker in the deep, sunken lanes around Ightham and Plaxtol there is a new peril, a hail of sticks and split conker shells followed by a horde of children in search of this year's potential champion.

Chestnut trees, both horse and Spanish, are a feature of the southeast countryside, in parks and woodlands, on village greens and lining the town streets. The Spanish or sweet chestnut introduced by the Romans ripens best in the south. The two largest specimens are both in the area, one 36 m giant in Godinton Park in Kent, and another with a girth of 8 m at Carshalton in Surrey. We can claim the two largest horse chestnuts, too, one in Surrey and on in Petworth Park. What did the small boys do before the horse chestnut was introduced from southern Europe early in the seventeenth century? Perhaps they used shells. One of the many interpretations of conker is derived from 'concha', a shell. But the boys who assaulted me, quite accidentally, in the hollow-way up to Oldbury Hill were sure it was something to do with the Conqueror or conking each other or something equally aggressive. One of the first recorded plantings of this tree was by a Kentish gardener, John Tradescant, in 1633.

October is for acorns and the fall of beech mast, those that the squirrels and wood pigeons have left behind. The brown acorns, some of them already reddening with young shoots at the base, can be as close packed as pebbles on a beach. Each leaf selects its own pattern of decay, some curling at the edges with fungal attack, others turning steadily from green to yellow and brown to the final russet-like flames in the forest. Much of the yellowing of oak leaves is caused by layers of spangle gall like decorative jewels underneath the leaf. They fall in October to mature on the ground and become next year's gall wasps. The galls can be nearly as prolific as birch seeds. The rowan leaves are as thin and delicate as yellowing parchment, the red seeds spattering the ground, yet even the rowan, as eye-catching in its time as the hawthorn in May, is outshone by the whitebeam, another characteristic tree of the chalk country. The berries are larger than the rowan, growing in large clusters. While the top surface of the large, oval leaf yellows, the underside is a downy white. When the wind blows, the whitebeam is a constantly changing curtain of colour. When it leafs in May, the whitebeam, one of the *sorbus* family, can be as lovely as a magnolia, but October witnesses its supreme visual display. The berries are edible when they begin to rot and have been used in various concoctions with wine and honey. The berries of the wild service tree, another *sorbus*, remain much greener but they, too, have been used for flavouring, one known recipe putting them in whisky. Most of the berries, especially those of the rowan, are rich in vitamin C and can be used for jellies.

The ideal setting for the delicate deciduous colours is a woodland where they can contrast with the darkness of yew and holly and a sombre backcloth of pine. Such a setting, together with a constantly changing vista of hill slope and river, can be found in the Mole Gap between Dorking and Leatherhead. On the one side, the tangle of yew and box on the steep river cliff called the Whites gives way on the crest to a mixed woodland. On the other lies the dark evergreen height of Ranmore Common, still with a fair quota of oak and beech and other deciduous trees. To the north of Ranmore is Norbury Park, famous for its Druid's Grove of ancient yews. Early topographers record the dotted chestnut moth in October here, gorged with the juice of yew berries. The woodland clearings on the summit of the park towards Fetcham Downs are a frequent haunt for green woodpeckers. The subtle tree-planting of Norbury is matched on the east bank of the Mole by the exotica around Juniper Hall, once famed for its fugitives from the French Revolution such as Talleyrand and Madame de Stael and now equally famous as one of the first field study centres in the country.

The steep slope of the valley backing Juniper Hall is covered with birch, yew, Scots pine and larch. The ingredients sound simple, but the colour contrasts of October transform that hill slope into a memorable patchwork, light yellow of birch, dark yew, light green of pine change subtly as the sun moves full arc across them. Most of the woodland in the area was planted by private landowners, such as the Duke of Athol, early in the nineteenth century. Prior to that time, the area was farmland. The earth banks of old field boundaries can be traced beneath the present woodland cover. Even Mickleham Down was farmed before it reverted to common. Conifers were planted extensively on the steep-sided valleys leading towards Headley, giving the area the name of Little Switzerland.

This part of Surrey is a training ground for students of landscape and contains some of the best and most heavily used open spaces in the south-east. Much of the land is protected, either by the National Trust, the Surrey Naturalists' Trust, the Field Studies Council and the local authority. Most of the hill area is classified as an 'area of outstanding natural beauty' and, in recent years, the area in the immediate vicinity of Box Hill has been designated as a 'country park'. Abundant footpaths and bridleways give access to both sides of the Mole Valley. The best link between them lies between Mickleham Church and Norbury Park, although the most romantic crossing is by the stepping stones about half a mile south of Burford Bridge. These stones lead to the Pilgrims' Way as it skirts round the foot of Box Hill. During summer drought, the Mole may be low enough to see some of the swallow holes in its bed where the surface water disappears underground. But copious autumn rains can make the crossing a much more adventurous experience.

Amonst the variety of woodland scenery are patches of open grassland such as Juniper Top where the last of the chalk flora still lingers, opening briefly in the rare sunshine. Most prominent are the field scabious and devil's bit scabious, the former having about fifty small flowers in a clustered head, one of the most copious suppliers of honey to insects and once a fashionable infusion for ladies determined to lose weight. A number of bellflowers are still in evidence, the harebell, the clustered bellflower and the deep blue nettle-leaved bellflower. The small yellow flowers of the rock-rose, conspicuous since the spring, are still opening afresh in the milder days of autumn.

In one such clearing, where the Roman Stane Street strides on its last stage to Epsom and London over Mickleham Down, I watched a fox moving slowly through the edge of beech woodland. He was moving in no special direction, turning over fallen branches, snuffling amongst the leaves, eating whatever tasty morsels he could find. Foxes, like badgers, enjoy the occasional fungus and on that damp, cool ground there were fungi in plenty. The big, fat, spongy cep, the giant horn of plenty, wood mushrooms, the poisonous yellow-oyster fungus, yellow chanterelle, white caps and shaggy ink caps. Bracket fungi stuck out like ears from a fallen birch tree with clusters of honey fungus near by. Two heads of fly agaric, red and bold, looked dangerously palatable. But my fox ignored most of them and seemed most interested in the grubs around the tree roots. With more than 10,000 different species of fungus and many of them edible, the beech woods of autumn become a culinary delight, but for me there is more than a hint of fear in the fascination of fungi. Many of them look singularly repellent. I leave them to the experts and to their major task in breaking down the debris of the forest floor, returning the nutrients to the soil.

Fungi are not confined to deciduous woodland. The nature reserve at Witley Common keeps a careful record of the fungi within its boundaries, bracket fungus, beef steak, death cap, fly agaric, parasol, chanterelle, blewits and several types of boletus. There are the champignons associated with fairy rings, on commons and heaths, that have sometimes been confused with the play-rings of deer. I heard a most interesting suggestion of a link between the activities of deer on their play-rings and the ergot fungus which affects purple moor grass. The argument went that the deer are attracted to the grass, eat it and then, affected by the fungus, run around in circles. I have no idea how scientific the observation was.

There is one such play-ring on the clearing on Mickleham Down. Encounters with wild deer are not uncommon there. I was once confronted with a large red hind only 9 m away. In the perpetual tension of the wild, she kept lowering and raising her head rhythmically as if trying to gauge the distance between us and the nature of the danger facing her. The extensive woodlands and heaths of Surrey and West Sussex provide good cover for feral deer on the move. It is not unusual to hear a crashing noise in a hawthorn thicket and find a buck thrashing with his antlers. Thrashing may be used to remove the last of the velvet hanging in strips from the antlers, but by early October it is also used for marking territory, a scent being left on the thrashed areas. Bucks may select one tree for special attention. A fallow buck, for example, may address a Scots pine for many minutes, licking it, muzzling it, rubbing its horns gently against it, rubbing it with cheek and throat, even with the back of the neck. The buck has other scent glands beneath the eyes and it may be anointing the tree with the scent. Such trees often exude their sticky sap and the worn areas of the bark show the results of such treatment over a long period of time.

Early autumn is a time of much activity in deer. Roe deer usually mate in August, but this is followed by a so-called false rut. The fallow deer mate in October with much fraying before and after and running in play-rings especially before the rut. Wild roe tend to move about the countryside in small family groups. A dozen of them, bucks and does and fawns, once crossed my path in full daylight on the South Downs Way moving from woodland below the escarpment near Beacon Hill over the open crest of the Downs to another covert at Marden. They were quite unconcerned except for three does at the back of the file which hesitated, looked towards me and then pranced after the rest with that extraordinary bouncing action with all four feet leaving the ground at once. Such groups usually lie up in cover during the day, in old quarries, in woods and even growing crops. Fallow and roe are the most common though there are occasional sightings of red deer and muntjac.

Most of the feral deer groups began as escapees from the many deer parks in the region. Maintaining the high fences and the deer herds became expensive luxuries, one of the first victims of the need for economy on the big estates. Cowdray, Uppark and Arundel, in

Sussex and Witley in Surrey are all examples. Occasional escapes take place from established parks such as Petworth. There is a notorious seven-year-old white buck at Knole who spends much of his time hanging around one of the gates looking for a chance to get out. He has been brought back from Sevenoaks High Street on more than one occasion.

Deer are amongst the most easily observed wild animals because of the survival of several deer parks and October is the most dramatic month in the annual cycle. The word 'park' has a domesticated ring about it and the deer in some places have become so used to visitors that they, too, are nearly tamed. Yet watch a fallow buck standing in a clearing throwing his head rhythmically backwards and forwards uttering harsh warning groans from his swollen throat trying to dominate his territory with his show of aggression. Other bucks in the vicinity answer him until the whole arena echoes like a battlefield. Sixteen does are cropping quietly near by until one suddenly breaks from the ring and bounds towards the woodland edge where another buck stands. The buck races after her, skidding in a sharp turn to head her off, butting her white inflated rump. She trots back, mewing plaintively. A young pricket approaches and the buck reacts violently. Another doe takes advantage of his distraction and escapes to another harem .The buck groans violently, beating his forelegs up and down in an exaggerated slow march like a soldier on parade. The restless energy of the rut can transform a quiet parkland scene into an agitated mass, a series of swirling circles of deer, stags racing and roaring through the herd, locking horns, eyes flaring. So competitive are the bucks, so concerned with the harem of does they are attracting that they have no time to feed. Even a master buck, apparently omnipotent in his 70 m or so of territory with fifty or more does close by, remains on guard standing in the middle, seldom resting. During the rut the bucks lose weight. Traditionally, the greater the wasting, the better the quality of venison later. The growth of antlers is related to the sexual drive and the time of the rut sees them at their finest. The finest to be seen in the region are on the stags of the red deer herd at Warnham in Sussex, a herd made famous by the paintings of J. G. Millais in the last century. The great house is now a school but the herd is maintained, the only herd of red deer apart from the royal herd in Richmond Park. During the summer, the magnificent stags rest quietly in the shade of old parkland oaks with their velvet hanging in shreds, like warriors hiding their wounded pride. By September they are once again the royal beasts of the forest, fit for kings.

The finest deer herd in the region is at Parham Park in Sussex. Selective breeding has produced a dark coated, almost black breed of fallow deer, its quality maintained by annual culling, sometimes nearly a half of the herd. Even in the driest of summers when other parks were driven in desperation to feed apples and oranges by the ton to their deer, Parham found enough natural grazing by keeping the numbers down. The bucks are culled in August and September before the rut, a selection of the older deer as well as young prickets being shot. The venison finds a good market on the continent. The does are culled in February, the total herd being kept at about two hundred. The fallow herd at Knole is twice as large but the Parham deer are wilder creatures, more difficult but more exciting to observe.

Petworth has a roe herd, the only one in the region, but they are seldom seen as they are a woodland deer and tend to remain in cover while the fallow herd, the largest in the country, grazes with the Sussex red cattle and the black sheep in the lovely natural bowl of the Upper Park, an immense open space broken only by the occasional chestnut and oak and clumps of beech and pine, many of them dating from the time of Capability Brown who introduced others of his favourite landscape devices such as the serpentine lake fronting the house. 'Percy to the core', said Walpole of Petworth, a reference presumably to its Northumbrian owners. Brown, too, was a Northumbrian by birth and the park brings more than a hint of the wildness of the Border country to the gentler airs of Sussex.

The antics of the deer, the subtle almost theatrical spacing of the trees, the sheer majesty of the setting with views encompassing Blackdown to the north and Chanctonbury to the south makes Petworth unique. An enclosure of the original Wealden wilderness, modified by Brown, immortalised by Turner who was a frequent visitor to the house, Petworth is one of the last examples of the picturesque, the artist's canvas spread on the grandest of scales, the landscape itself.

Whether Parham or Petworth, Knole or Buxted, wherever there are deer there always seem to be fly-catchers hurtling from fallen trees or low branches to grab a passing insect and then speeding back as if attached to a piece of elastic. I have seen both the pied and the spotted fly-catchers so occupied in the autumn parks though they have usually migrated by October. The hobby, too, one of the smaller falcons, frequents Parham and Petworth on his late summer forays. The bird's limited breeding area includes this part of West Sussex. Other parkland birds are woodpeckers and meadow pipits, the latter usually in flocks often on passage. Inevitably the starlings are feeding close to the deer. They will even perch on a deer's back, walk along the spine and right down the sloping neck to the snout. They are gathering flies and insects which are attracted to the deer, though some of their antics suggest that they are enjoying the routine like a slide in the park. Pied wagtails and magpies also get in on the act. There are marsh tits clambering about the dying stems of bracken, robins singing brightly again from the hawthorns and suddenly a late, lone swallow sweeps along the glade where the deer are, for the moment, at peace.

There are parks and gardens without deer herds that are open to the public in October and receive many visitors just because of the sheer beauty of tree colour, especially where exotica like the many varieties of Japanese maple and acers add their incredible crimsons. Most of the famous gardens, like Nymans, Sheffield Park, Scotney and Sissinghurst are open for at least the first part of the month, but some privately owned gardens open under the National Garden scheme. Hole Park, owned by the Barham family, near Rolvenden in Kent, is one of the best, its dell garden being the most glorious of its many favours. Winkworth Arboretum, in the Surrey hills near Godalming, is open all the year round, but it rightly claims its peak display to be towards the end of the month. Yet even the leafy delicacies of Hole Park or Winkworth cannot match the sheer abundance of Bedgebury.

The exotica there turn the last days of October into a painter's dreamland, defying the straight lines of the experimental plots, turning the damp corner of the Weald into a magic microcosm of the world. Individually the trees are a wonder, but the conjunction of colour and shape makes the pinetum a work of art. The small divided leaf of the gingko hangs like a creamy yellow fan in front of a curtain of dark cypress. Tulip trees hold up their remarkably shaped leaves alongside a plot of Chilean pines. Scarlet oaks from the eastern seaboard of the USA confront the rusty barks of Scots pine. Chestnut brown leaves from Hungarian oaks fall on to branches of Norway spruce.

The floor of the pinetum is matchless. Each step shows a new wonder. In sheer size none outspans the sycamore. In colour none matches the wild service tree, a true native, with fine red veins in a green palmate leaf. Yet another leaf from the same tree shows green veins in a red leaf. These are colours to shame even the goldcrests and long-tailed tits that are working along the branches, dislodging leaves as they go and adding their mite to the general riot of October's unexcelled beauty.

CHAPTER 11

November

Whether it be souling, burning the Guy, clemmening, catterning or going St Andring, November persists with ritual and dark celebration, fire and woodsmoke in garden and village green. For our Saxon forebears, founders of our village homesteads, it was 'blot-monath', the month of sacrifice with ritual oxen killed for the pagan gods. The gods changed to saints and the celebrations kept on, All Saints and All Souls, St Clements, St Catherine and St Andrew. Since the nineteenth century the power of the saints has receded, too, and Guy Fawkes became the central figure of November's fires, and the sadness of the season found a new reflection in the remembrance of the dead, Armistice Day. And even that day coincides with the opening of the month in the old calendar.

When the sparkling wheels spin on the fifth they recall also a

November saint, St Catherine whose day, the 25th, was celebrated by children begging for apples and pears. Hence, the catterning. Two days before was the day of St Clements when the smiths fired their anvils with the judicious addition of a little gunpowder to heighten the effect. Then they went from house to house in Sussex demanding apples and beer. Fruit was a persistent theme, always fresh from the late harvest, some apples and pears still on the trees.

Fire, too, persists in most of the festivals, burning up the debris of autumn, clearing the way for winter. Some villages, like Edenbridge, make a great public display of fireworks whereas the small, picturesque village of Ightham has most cause, having in its fine stone church a memorial tomb dedicated to the memory of Dame Selby who, according to the inscription, 'disclosed' the Gunpowder Plot. How or where she discovered it is uncertain. Some historians maintain that she merely depicted it in her famous embroidery. A copy hangs in the church illustrating the conspirators, the Pope and a devil with horns. Ightham, like so many villages in the region, has a collection of timber-framed buildings that date back beyond the date of the plot. Perhaps an incautious word was overheard in one of those great fireplaces or in a secret tunnel curling down towards the stream. Such legends are the stuff of village histories.

The great celebration is at Lewes, ancient country town of Sussex which still remembers its seventeen Protestant martyrs. Its method of remembrance with barrels of burning pitch recalls a much older custom such as the bonfires of midwinter. Even the word Guy finds an echo in the older guisers, men with blackened faces, in disguise, so to speak, who burned the great fires in the heart of winter darkness. The bonfire boys of Lewes had so fierce a reputation that lovers of law and order often tried to stop such goings-on. Tarring and feathering were all part of the nineteenth-century antics. This is traditionally the day when the herrings arrive off the Sussex coast, according to local fishermen, in order to see the fireworks, so they had additional cause for celebration.

The older celebration of St Clements, patron saint of the smiths, complete with effigy, was maintained in villages like Burwash until late in the nineteenth century. Burwash was one of the many villages and small towns of the Weald in which the iron industry was important. A fine iron tomb plate is embedded in one of the internal walls of the church and Rudyard Kipling's home at

Batemans was an ironmaster's house in the seventeenth century. Even the name of the local inn, 'The Bear', may be a reference to the industry which made the valleys ring with forge and furnace. The 'bears' were lumps of unfused iron drawn out of the furnace floors and discarded. They can be anything up to a metre across, a mixture of iron and stone, sometimes still gleaming with a metallic sheen. They are usually found near the dams or 'bays' at the mouth of the hammer ponds that supplied the water power for the industry. They may supply the doorstep of an old cottage as at the Priest's House at West Hoathly or be found underneath the floors of barns. 'Sows' and 'pigs' are lumps of iron ready for resmelting and forging into wanted shapes like cannons and balls, firebacks, tombs and railings. Throughout the Weald names like Furnace Farm and Forge Cottage occur abundantly as far west as Abinger Hammer in Surrey or at Horsted Keynes on the edge of Ashdown Forest where one of the best flights of 'ponds' can be reached by footpath north of the church. In the same area is Buxted, once home of Master Hogg who forged the first cannon. The heraldic snout of the hog still stands on the wall of the Dutch-gabled house at the entrance to Buxted Park.

Six miles or so south of Burwash in East Sussex is Ashburnham, the last stronghold of the industrial age of the Weald, where iron was worked right up to the nineteenth century, long after the Carron Company of Clydeside had taken the naval contracts which had made the Weald famous. Two large sows stand by the gateposts of Forge Cottage. A bridleway leads north from the cottage across pastures to the site of the furnace where the dam is capped with slag and cinder. Even the stepping stones across the stream above the dam are 'bears'. The path leads on up the valley, the woodland on either side being pitted with deep holes where the nodules of iron ore were extracted from the thick Wealden clay. The extensive parkland, fashioned by Capability Brown, that lies around the mansion of Ashburnham, recalls the industrial wealth that enabled some of the greatest houses of the region to be built and rebuilt. Iron from these areas, only six miles fron the Roman coastal fort at Pevensey, equipped the Roman channel fleet and experts have been able to identify the earliest smelting sites, the bloomeries, simple circular floors in the woodlands, identified by the slag and cinder found nearby. Such material can be seen on the surfaces of Roman roads as at Holtye Common near Cowden, another centre of the industry. In Pevensey Castle itself stands one of the cannons forged at Robertsbridge. Cannons are few, but firebacks are many. Most of the great houses have several firebacks of local workmanship, so do local inns and old cafés. Local museums at Battle, Hastings and Lewes have interesting collections.

One of the most dramatic memorials of the industry is to be found on the floor of Wadhurst Church. The floor rings as you walk across it. And no wonder, for there are no less than thirty-one iron tomb slabs set amongst the flagstones and tiles. The dates range from 1617 to 1747. The Barhams of Snape and the Saunders of Pell have attained an immortality beyond stone. Their names, manors and devices are as proud as the day they were forged. A modern inheritor of the village craft tradition has filled the tower arch with a modern screen of mild steel and glass depicting the anvil, hammer, pincers and other images of the industry, together with a host of rural symbols, including the Sussex martlets, lambs, hops. The anvil occurs again together with the oast house in the village sign, one of the many fine metal signs in the region. Snape Wood, south of Wadhurst, was one of the last places where iron was extracted, though the evidence lies hidden under new conifer plantations.

Some of the hammer ponds filling the narrow wooded valleys are more than half a mile long. These water surfaces are being dwarfed by new reservoirs such as Weirwood, near East Grinstead, and Bewl Bridge, near Lamberhurst, which are taking advantage of the high rainfall of the High Weald and the impermeability of the soil that helped fill the first hammer ponds 400 years ago. Summer droughts often hindered the iron industry, but by November the streams are brimful, bouncing merrily from the high ridges down to their junctions with the main rivers.

Water was power for more than just the iron industry. It was the major source for most early settlements. The Domesday survey records nearly as many water mills as it does villages. More than 400 were still working, probably on the same sites as their medieval forebears, in the nineteenth century. Most of the sites can still be identified, often occupied by ruined mills. There has been a great revival of interest in recent years, witness the restoration of Woods Mill near Henfield. A water museum has been opened at Haxted on the Kent–Surrey border, open to the public until the end of October. The upper floor of the mill holds a collection of materials from the

Wealden iron industry. Another mill at nearby Edenbridge is in the process of restoration, depending on funds.

The water-mills have served more than one industry, corn grinding, iron hammering and cloth fulling. Some of the paper mills along the river Len near Maidstone are using sites that were once connected with the local cloth industry. Mills along the Tillingbourne in Surrey were connected with the manufacture of gunpowder. Part of the family fortune of the Evelyns at Albury came from this material trade. Two mills along that river are open occasionally to the public, the one at Gomshall and the National Trust mill at Shalford.

Wherever there are hammer ponds and the evidence of forge or furnace, there will be another characteristic feature of the south-eastern countryside, the coppiced woodlands. Trees cut down to the base or scrub send up copious shoots which grow within a dozen or more years into branches stout enough for poles. Leave them for another five years and they are tall and tough enough for hop supports. This specialised form of woodland management is much older than the hop fields and was used as an insurance for a plentiful supply of industrial fuel when restrictions were placed on the cutting of the big timbers which were needed for the shipyards. Chestnut supplies most of the coppices, but oak, ash, birch, hornbeam, hazel, beech, even cherry, were cut over in the same manner.

Though there is a declining demand for coppiced timber, there are many parts of the region where the cants or corners of woodland will be auctioned off in late October ready for the cutting to begin in November. All the bigger standard trees, even shrubs like holly and yew, must be left untouched but the rest of the ware is to be 'cut from the stub', to quote the auctioneer's words, by the end of March. Throughout the winter a small hut or lean-to, like a nomadic dwelling, appears in the woodlands giving shelter to the cutters and their tools. The sound of the power saws rings through the cold air, though some estates still insist on the use of handsaws. Then the barks are stripped off with specially curved knives for the poles last longer in the ground without their protective barks. Finally, the spiles for the fences are made by splitting the poles in two with a tool called a dill axe. Some coppicers can remember cutting for charcoal burning, especially the slow-burning hornbeam.

Thes ound of the saw is not the only sound to rend the November air. The hedge-cutter is at work, the municipal machine scraping along the roadsides giving an indiscriminate cropping to the old boundaries. At one time, hedges were trimmed back to produce new growth at the base of the shrubs so as to thicken up the hedges and make them more of a barrier to livestock. Young saplings of oak, elm and ash were carefully nurtured so as to supply the hedgerow timber of the future. Such trees supplied about one-third of the total supply of the region. Now the hedge is treated as something of a hindrance to be kept in check with the minimum effort, its timbers singed and shorn. Yet the hedges are not only an integral part of man's contribution to the landscape, marking the stages of his dominance over the wild, but one of the most attractive features of the autumn scene. A typical hedgerow of the Weald is composed of hawthorn, with holly, hazel and maple and occasional saplings of oak, ash and an invading elder. These boundaries date back to Tudor times when many medieval estates were being divided up for crop farming and the new breed of yeoman farmers was emerging from the ranks of the medieval tenants.

The November hedgerow, especially in the chalk country, is a major attraction for birds. Some of the boundaries associated with Saxon parishes and along old trackways have as many as two dozen different species of tree and shrub in them, many of them bearing a bounty of berries. Black clusters of dogwood and privet, the fat sloes of blackthorn, bright red of guelder rose and the darker red of hawthorn are all abundant. Whitebeam and the wayfaring tree have probably lost their crop by now and the holly is yet to reach its colourful climax. The flesh of yew berries, reputedly eaten by at least seventeen different species of bird, is spattered on the ground, but there is plenty for all. Even some blackberries are still appearing with a late crop of pink blossom shivering on the same thorny stem.

From tree-top to the ground, the hedges are bustling with birds. Blue tits sweep across the track for a hurried inspection of an ash tree while chaffinches swoop on a hawthorn disturbing a quiet family of goldcrests. With every flurry of birds, a shower of leaves falls, the ash in twigfuls, still green, the hawthorn in slow descent and the sycamore, as big as a fist, bounces on the wind. Blackbirds shuffling amongst the litter explode from the darker depths in rapid flight to a new haven, but the song thrush perched on the very summit of an oak launches into song, more like a herald of spring than a lament for autumn. Not to be outdone, a robin chooses a vantage point on the holly bush to show that he, too, has regained his voice. Most of the common birds include some berries in their diet and there are always the seeds of ash, maple, sycamore, hazel catkins, beech mast and acorns for a change of diet. The berries attract the winter migrants like fieldfare and redwing and, in hard times, the waxwing from the cold north.

The birds in their plundering help to propagate the shrubs and any uncultivated ground near such hedges and shaws shows the effect in a forest of young seedlings rising from the grasses and wild flowers. The hawthorn is the most successful of the plants, with privet and dogwood strong competitors. The barren stems of elder become smothered with Jew's ear fungus, a dark brown, limp growth that is soft and pliable as an ear in its early growth. Banded fungus grows for the hazel and the dead stems of birch are bandaged with a light frugal growth.

As the month toils on, many of the plants lose their splendour, but there is one small tree, rarely found outside the chalk country of the south, that emerges from its summer obscurity to become more and more prominent with delicate clusters of pinky-red capsules splitting to reveal four bright orange seeds. The fruits of the spindle tree may hang on long after the oval leaves have turned coppery brown, curled and fallen. The slender trunk and branches of the spindle are not notable, lost in the thorny thickets, yet that slender timber is one of the toughest of them all, strong enough to make spindles, knitting needles and pegs, hence its local names of prickwood, pegwood and skewerwood. The spindle is food for the larvae of the holly blue butterfly and is the winter host to the eggs of the black bean aphid, one of the reasons why some farmers try to eradicate it from their boundaries. You often have to be content with finding only one or two spindle trees in a day's walking, but there is a healthy copse of them growing by the main ride across the top of Mickleham Down north of Box Hill.

Another tree commonly found on chalk soils with a name to match the hardness of its wood is the hornbeam. At first sight both its leaf and its trunk can be mistaken for the beech, but its trunk is so fluted that it gives the impression of living muscles trapped beneath the bark. There is no mistaking the hornbeam in November. Its seed capsules hang down in clusters of horned wings, each holding a dark green seed. They can be so plentiful that the tree, seen in silhouette against a darkening sky, looks as if it is still in leaf. The seeds lie in the wet soil for eighteen months before germinating. Only the toughest of beaks like that of the hawfinch can attack the hornbeam seed. The timber is tough enough to make cog wheels in mills and for the yokes of oxen, hence its local name of yoke-beam. It still finds a use for butchers' chopping blocks and mallets. It has been coppiced for the purest charcoal, for the timber burns with the hottest flame of any tree. Hornbeams are often found in deer parks, usually pollarded, cut down to within about ten feet of the ground, sending up a multitude of branches. Pollarding, like coppicing, was a form of tree management that gave a greater total yield of timber, though another explanation of the practice is that it kept the branches out of reach of livestock. Deer are partial to hornbeam leaves.

The most typical boundary of the south-east is not the hedgerow but the shaw, a name that occurs time and again on the large-scale maps. The word is related to the Scandinavian word for wood "skog" and defines the broad strips of woodland that were left standing when the first fields were cleared. Rights-of-way frequently thread through them. They may occupy as much as a third of the land surface in some parishes especially where the forest was lately colonised as on the plateau tops of the North Downs, above Wrotham, for example, or in the clay vales around Pluckley and Bethersden. As the shaws are relics of a medieval pattern of farming so their flora reveal all the variety of native trees and shrubs. The shaws are sanctuaries and highways for wildlife and the ground is often pockmarked by badger setts, fox earths and rabbit burrows. Some of the deep scratches and shallow pits are the result of pheasants and other game birds grubbing for seeds and insects for this is one of their favourite nesting sites.

The hedges and shaws, valuable as historic record and wildlife reserves, are suffering especially in areas of new arable farming. They have virtually disappeared from the South Downs, though a recent survey showed that Sussex as a whole had about 10 per cent of such cover. Now they are being grubbed up on the heavier clay-with-flint soils capping the North Downs. Above Boxley and Hollingbourne, the hedged landscape has been transformed in one decade into broad ploughed fields that would not be out of place in East Anglia. The ancient Ridgeway, possibly the oldest track in the region, has been obliterated in long stretches.

NOVEMBER

The loss of hedgerows is not just a loss for wildlife but also for the wild flowers that linger on in their shade long after the main flowering season has closed. Red campion, red clover, self heal, sow thistle, scarlet pimpernel, scentless mayweed, rough hawkbit and smooth hawksbeard, wall lettuce and even a few heads of herb bennet may be encountered along the wayside enjoying the last dribbles of warmth from the old year. One of the most cherished late flowers that may be recorded in every month of the year is Herb Robert, a flower for all seasons and a remedy for all ills. Its delicate palmate leaves are edged with crimson, but its five pink petals still fresh as summer. One of the geranium family, its crushed seed heads were used for green wounds. It staunched bleeding, cured sore throats, nephritis, piles, ulcers, a cure-all much used on medieval battlefields. It has been known since the thirteenth century, appearing in a medieval treatise dedicated to Robert, Duke of Normandy.

Dry stone walls are a rarity throughout the region although there is plentiful stone available. Occasionally flint walls are found enclosing paddocks and intakes close to farms and there are many brick walls surrounding gardens from the seventeenth century. Some, as at Kemsing, have been built into the curious fashion of crinkle-crankle, a zig-zag device that gives an even greater length facing the south with ample nooks for floral shelter. Such walls, even in November, can support a surprising number of flowers such as dandelion, valerian, yellow corydalis, hairy bittercress, rue-leaved saxifrage, common field speedwell, abundant mosses and ferns and garden plants like antirrhinum escaping over the retaining wall. The lime used as mortar adds a new nutrient to the 'soils' and the heat stored in the wall gives a longer season to the flowers.

Even without such a floral cover, walls can be a work of art, due to the tradition of galletting. Small chips of stone are embedded into the mortar, helping to bind it and acting as a protection against birds looking for nesting sites in wall crannies. Whatever its initial function, galletting has a highly decorative effect. It is most prominent in West Sussex where large flint flakes are stuck into the thick mortar needed to keep the angular lumps of flint together. The system of mortaring has local names such as snail creep. Some of the walls on the Goodwood Estate, for example, have such massive flakes that they look positively hostile. Most effective of all are the small, brown chips of ironstone used in sandstone walls looking like lines of beads traced round the stonework. A regional variation found in the fold country of Surrey, at Alford, for example, places the stone chips in such a way that they look like large nail heads studding the walls, not dissimilar in effect to the iron nails used in some of the local oak doors in churches.

By November, the sheep flocks with their yearlings have left the hedgeless, wind-swept levels of Romney and other marshes, made even more bleak by the continuing loss of the elms, for the more sheltered valleys of the inland area and the orchard country. Not that they seem too comforted with the rain hanging over the Wealden hills like a wet blanket, clouds hanging in the trees like smoke. It only needs a little rain to turn the heavy clays into a morass and the autumn often brings it in abundance. October and November are the two wettest months in the High Weald, which has nearly twice the rain of the coastal areas. With little warm sun to evaporate the moisture, the soils become waterlogged. Ploughing and sowing have to wait for the right days. Pastoral farming is still the rule in the small grassy intakes in the valleys. The sheep and cattle poach the grass into porridge. The bite is soft and poor and the beasts graze on unexpected things like hedges, scoffing chestnuts, even to the spiky c? , and shovel up acorns by the slavering mouthful. Such a c an have disastrous results, causing blockages in the intestines a. possible death. To add to the frustrations, the hunt hurrahs over the hills, descends bravely through the drifting rain, stampedes the livestock and does no good at all to the fences. The farmer moves the herds into the quieter corners waiting to run the rams with the ewes and put the impatient bull to his cows. ready for next spring's progeny.

Machines are almost a hindrance in conditions like this. A farmer at Sadlescombe has maintained shire horses as part of his farm museum, together with a marvellous collection of old ploughs, implements and photographs of the days that are gone. But the horses have proved more than a museum piece. They work wet soils and awkwardly shaped fields better than an unwieldy machine, especially on lifting potatoes. I watched a giant machine groping across a large flat field in the North Kent market gardening area with six men huddled inside it sorting out the potatoes from the stones, a rural scene as bleak as a factory belt. There seemed to be as many good potatoes crushed into the wet soil as the machine had unearthed. Old practices are not always outdated, so good luck to the Sedlescombe farmer who adds to his enterprise with farm museum and nature trails as well as his pick-your-own seasons, in the more fruitful days of summer. I don't think he will ever find a use for the Kentish turn-wrist plough in his collection, an implement so heavy that even eighteenth-century writers on agriculture commented on its size and said that it had timber in it to make a Highland cart. That great plough was still in use in this century, dragged by a team of eight oxen. So full of locally wrought iron and tough oak beams as to be a symbol of the region, the plough was the only implement that could work the heavier Wealden soils. There are specimens lying in odd corners of the region, by the roadside at Ruckinge, on the roof of the 'Plough Inn' at Trottiscliffe as well as the small farm museums, a fearsome plough that must have bred ploughmen as tough as oxen to hold it to the furrow.

Now the rooks are flocking, the gulls moving in from the coasts and the roosts of starlings building up into black, wheeling clouds over the bare trees. On the ploughed fields the peewits rummage around, cleaning the ground of insects and grubs, especially the leather-jackets. The peewit was once the farmer's friend in more ways than one for its flesh was esteemed as good food in the winter months. Its wheeling, acrobatic flight and its haunting cry makes it one of the most distinctive birds of the month with its names of lapwing or peewit. Its third name, the plover, has been associated with the French 'pluvier', to rain, and it is certainly active in the wet season, notably when the ground is beginning to thaw after night frost. The insects become active. So does the peewit. The group name for peewits is a 'deceit', presumably a reference to their habit of feigning injury to draw intruders away from nesting sites. The autumn flocks can reach 500 or 600 birds in one black mass. When they are joined, as is often the case, with rooks and gulls and starlings and a mob of the smaller finches and tits and sparrows, the effect is majestic. The cause of such flocking is not fully understood, whether for company or security or warmth. The effect is to transform a dying month with the liveliest of displays.

CHAPTER 12

December

A cold coming they had of it, the Pilgrims, just the wrong time of the year. Becket was martyred in the last week of the year and the true pilgrimage had to be undertaken in the cold and damp of the dark days to reach Canterbury for the Feast of St Thomas. The traditional route followed the line of the Old Way from Winchester to Canterbury that threaded its muddy ways along the foothills of Surrey and Kent, a route taken by the penitent King, Henry II, in four days and later by modern stalwarts like Hilaire Belloc, eight days on foot, tracing and retracing his steps in the quest for the one true path. The earlier pilgrims were warmed by the ancient December fairs that were organised, as at Guildford, to cater for the new travellers. It was not until the later fourteenth century that the summer pilgrimages became popular and led to the decline of the winter fairs.

Along the Way were churches like jewels on a necklace, some, as at Seale, specially built to attract the wayfarers. Tolls were exacted, relics were sold, exotic goods vended from the booths. There were many wonders on the Way long before Canterbury was reached. The unique double chancel at Compton, built in about 1180, the Martyrs' Hill near Guildford, the chalybeate Spring of St Edith at Kemsing, the miraculous Rood and image of St Rumbold at Boxley, the block of wood on which St John the Baptist was beheaded kept at Charing on the Archbishop's estate. For the wealthier pilgrims there were palaces, castles and abbeys at convenient stages at Farnham, at Guildford, at Reigate, at Otford, at Wrotham and Charing.

In following that route the pilgrims were using a cross-country road already hallowed by time, a track threading its way between the high, windswept downs and the damp lowlands, a track that had been in use since the New Stone Age. Some called it the tin route, used for trade by the Phoenicians. The Romans knew it well and lined it with their villas. Along it they found the great stones and tombs of civilisations as old to them as the Romans are to us. The Old Way is not just a journey through 4,000 years of history, but a walk through a belt of countryside sufficiently attractive to be protected in modern times as an 'area of outstanding natural beauty'. In winter the barrenness of the trees and the dying back of the undergrowth reveals new aspects of that beauty as well as the tell-tale marks of the past, deserted villages and old stones that tease the imagination.

By a quirk of history, the Old Way became abandoned as a major highway along much of its length, leaving long stretches as country lanes, green tracks and footpaths. Such paths are the basis of the modern long-distance walkway, the North Downs Way, ideal for the modern country explorer willing to brave the slippery chalky paths, relishing the shelter of the hoary trees and shrubs that still line so much of the Way, shelter and food for birds, foxes, rabbits and the abundant smaller fauna getting ready for the siege of winter.

Early writers have all commented on the ancient yew trees that are found along the entire route, some using them as guidelines when the alignment of the Way became doubtful. Fanciful stories were invented about travellers who died on the journey having their graves marked by such trees, but yews are native to the chalk country and they are more likely to be remnants of the old wood-land cover, easily propagated by the seeds dispersed by the birds. None the less, the sense of antiquity along the Way is heightened by the persistent presence of the native evergreen that became a symbol of immortality.

For December walking, the easiest miles are those that approach the region from the west in Surrey for they lie not on the slopes of the chalk, but on the drier, better drained ridge of sandstone that runs to the south of the Downs. Between Farnham and Guildford and, again, from Guildford eastwards as far as Shere, the feet of the pilgrims would have been powdered with sand rather than caked with white chalky mud. A line of churches, Seale, Puttenham, Compton and St Martha's on the Hill lie on or near this more southerly route. Even in Kent, the alignment of churches, often known as Pilgrims' churches, is a good half-mile to the south of the Way. There are very few churches or settlements at all on the Way itself. So the modern pilgrim has many historic puzzles to occupy him on the long miles. The way is much older than the churches and the villages that owe their origin to our Saxon forebears and our Norman masters.

From Farnham to Puttenham the Way is used by surfaced roads but from Puttenham to St Martha's there are eight miles of good walking country on a narrow zone of Surrey heathland, with abundant conifers like the Scots pine joining the yew and holly as evergreen images appropriate to the time of the year. A hard frost glistening on the morning ground or a light flecking of snow trans-forms the land with new beauty, a cold coming but a spectacular one.

The pilgrims were easily diverted from their strict route and so is the modern country walker in search of new interests. Just a mile to the south-west of Puttenham village is one of Surrey's fine open spaces, Puttenham Common, a small but diverse area of steep, heathery slopes and deep valleys lined with ponds large enough to deserve the name of lakes. There is gorse in bloom there even in the hardest days, a plant that was once used as winter fodder, as thatch on poorer cottages, as a source of dyes. Even the dying fronds of bracken turn a rich coppery colour in the low sun almost as lovely as the last leaves of the beech trees with the sun shining through them. A flock of unseen starlings suddenly bursts out of a holly bush scattering the berries in their chattering flight.

Down on the ponds, the mallards are cackling with wintry humour as eight of their number circle the frozen surface three times before making a tentative landing, sliding to an undignified halt on the wet ice. Long-tailed tits scatter seeds from the birch tree where the stubby female catkins are breaking up, scattering the small horn-shaped seeds all over the common. On the lower branches of an alder trapped in the frozen pond a wren skulks with low secretive flight from cover to cover. Hunting the cutty wren was one of the traditions of December, often on Boxing Day. The little king or the hedge king, as he was called, was beaten from the hedges and carried in procession, adorned with oak and mistletoe, a custom possibly as old as the Way itself, yet one that was carried on in parts of the region until the last century.

A kestrel drifts silently out of the mist and perches momentarily on a low branch overlooking the lake. The heathlands are important winter feeding grounds for many birds of prey and there is always a chance of seeing something rather rarer than the kestrel such as the hen harrier, the buzzard and even a great grey shrike with its black piratic mask, all of which have been recorded on the near-by heaths in December. In winter, too, the kingfisher is much more conspicuous with short bursts of low, dipping flight and brilliant display of metallic blue. The kingfisher, a much smaller bird than one imagines, needs open water and is often more abundant on coasts and estuaries in winter, but many keep to the rivers like the Mole and the Wey while the waters are still open. Kingfishers, like herons and other fish-eating birds, suffer a heavy loss of numbers during severe winters.

Back on the Way the good walking starts by the footpath opposite 'The Jolly Farmers' and, typical of Surrey, encounters a golf course, a pilgrims' cottage, first of the many, and opulent detached houses hiding discreetly on the heathland. After two miles the village of Compton needs another short diversion to the south but it is worth it for the church of St Nicholas, patron saint of travellers, retains many features that would have been familiar to the early pilgrims. Its tower and chancel of flint and ironstone rubble, its anchorite cell, its massive Norman font and the unique two-storeyed sanctuary protected by one of the oldest wooden screens in the country, all survive to this day. The glass fragments of Madonna and Child in the east wall make the perfect visual focus of the architectural gem, craftsmanship in every piece of stone, glass and wood. There is still a hive of craftsmen operating in the area as well as a gallery devoted to a Victorian artist, G. F. Watts.

Three miles further on the Old Way crosses the river Wey at Shalford, site of one of the greatest of medieval fairs and now a growing town on the outskirts of Guildford. It holds a memory of yet another pilgrim, John Bunyan, who lived in the vicinity and may have based his Vanity Fair on that of Shalford. The common where the fair was held is only an isolated patch in the big arable fields of Surrey's better farming land spreading across the gentler slopes of the Downs. This was once hop country, too, and an occasional oast may be encountered. The route reaches its height both scenically and topographically as it rises from the east bank of the Wey through woodlands still bearing their medieval name of the Chantries, to the sandy heights of St Martha's, one of the most isolated churches in the region. St Martha's is almost certainly a corruption of 'martyrs'; a special chapel was added to the earlier church by the prior of Newark for the pilgrim trade. The walls of the church and churchyard are constructed of the tough, angular fragments of ironstone that occur in the local sandstone and look especially attractive in low sunlight. The view from the top of the hill is impressive, northwards to the Downs, southwards to the wilds of Blackheath and the Wealden forest beyond which was still comparatively unknown, a frontier of settlement when the pilgrims passed. Often the December scene is circumscribed by mist emphasising the sense of isolation. Silhouettes of yew and holly, pine and oak shiver in the low cloud with bracken dripping with moisture, heather and bilberry still surprisingly green. The croak of unseen birds makes them all sound like omens and one can imagine the pilgrims gathering into closer groups, aware of the dangers of the winter passage, before descending the yellow track to the east. An alternative route lay to the north of the hill along the valley by Tyting Farm, a big farm with modern buildings bearing an early Saxon name. The two routes are joined by footpaths which make together a very good short circuit of pilgrim country for three or four miles of winter walking, not spoilt by the new conifer plantations on the Chantries, a woodland now controlled by the corporation of Guildford.

East of Shere the exact alignment of the Way becomes doubtful, most authorities accepting the route slightly northwards to reach the foot of the Downs, near Newlands Corner. The next good walking section starts by the stepping stones over the river Mole just to the south of Burford Bridge hugging the foot of Box Hill through a tangle of box trees, hawthorn, privet, dogwood, spindle, yew, blackthorn, holly and wayfaring trees. The wayfaring tree reputedly gained its name from the shade it gave to travellers in the hot days of summer, but even in winter it is remarkable, holding on to its fat leaves covered with white hairs on the underside well into the winter. Next year's flowers and leaves are already forming, an early promise of better days to come. The branches of the hoarwithy as it was called were used for tying up bundles, very useful no doubt to pilgrims loaded up from the Surrey fairs. At this point the Way forms a dividing line between the wildscape to the north and the farmland below. In earlier days parts of the Way were regarded as the northern boundary of the Weald. To the south, the pioneer farmers were freed of woodland tithes.

Just to the south lies Dorking, and Dorking was famous for snails. The local inns were renowned for their culinary delights and especially the large, fat Dorking snails, better known as Roman snails. Perhaps the Romans introduced the edible snail to England, although they are yet another feature that has been attributed to the pilgrims. Whatever their origin, the large snails, up to 5 cm in length, are often found along the Way though in winter they hibernate in crevices of wood or stone or find warmth under logs or leaf litter or even by digging themselves into the soil, covering their aperture with a membrane made of lime, just like closing the front door, to keep the draught out. Snail shells are mostly composed of calcium carbonate so the chalk downs are the habitat for many species of snail, so many and so varied that some species are named after villages where they are found, such as Luddesdown in Kent. December is the wrong month for gathering live snails, but the rabbits are still actively burrowing in the old banks along the track and one fresh excavation can reveal as many as twelve different types of shell. Hedge snails, hairy garden snails, banded sheep snail, the white almost transparent shell of the Kentish snail and the tiny pigmadeum. Rabbits are useful archaeologists; their burrowing may turn up fragments of mussel shell and ancient flint chips. Some of the flint mines of primitive man on the Sussex Downs were indicated by materials thrown up by rabbits and moles.

A more recent relic of industrial archaeology is found at the foot of Box Hill in the form of small brick kilns, usually at the entrance of disused lime quarries. There is a good example on Hackhurst Downs and at least one near Boxhurst. The hillside kilns gained an updraught of air which kept the furnaces going, burning the lime for building materials or for leading out to the fields. This is a tortuous part of the Way following the undulations of the Downs past Buckland as far as Colley Hill, a large open space owned by the National Trust, much visited on winter days by the people of Reigate just to the south. One of the interesting features of the Reigate skyline is the restored windmill on Reigate Heath, close by the golf house, one of hundreds that used to whirr round in winter's winds, churning the harvested corn into flour but now a rare survivor.

For many miles in its course through Holmesdale, the vale leading across the Surrey–Kent border, the Old Way makes tedious going, partly because it is surfaced for modern transport and partly because its old alignment was cut and diverted by landowners powerful enough to enclose large areas of countryside to make themselves a park more fitting as a setting for their new mansions. Titsey is one, Chevening another, both fashioned in the late eighteenth century, the latter the work of the Courthopes whose formal park and gardens were much admired by the greatest in the land. The mansion, one of several attributed to Inigo Jones, has been restored to its former grandeur recently as the home of the present Prince of Wales. There is a public right-of-way through the parkland, but the North Downs Way has been diverted on to the crest of the hill, following the even more ancient Ridgeway. This has one great visual advantage in giving a view through the famous key-hole, a cutting through the ring-belt of woodland so contrived as to frame the house from afar. Though much of the parkland has been ploughed up, the whole composition still reflects the landscape aspirations of two hundred years ago.

Holly is abundant throughout the way-side shaws, but it is worth special note in this area as it gave its name to the vale of Holmesdale. One of Britain's few native evergreens, the holly protects its thick leaves from grazing animals by developing spiky edges though it is possible to find plenty of leaves without them. The unusual foliage and the bright clusters of winter berries made it a centre of attraction even in pagan times, but it soon became linked with the Christian symbols of crucifixion and the crown of thorns. We can imagine the pilgrims gathering sprays on their winter journey. But birds like the holly berries, too, and they can strip a bush in a few days. A friend of mine once watched a blackbird gather fifteen berries in a minute or two hardly bothering to move along the branch. The frost often softens the berries, making them pappy and easier to eat. By its nature, the holly makes a better hedgerow than almost any other plant, and at Tandridge in Holmesdale is a circular holly hedge completely enclosing the churchyard and the largest yew tree in Britain.

The eighteenth-century landscape gardeners introduced an exotic tree from the Mediterranean region that had leaves with characteristics similar to those of the holly, but a tree that would grow into an even finer crown and dominate the winter woodland, the holm oak, or ilex. Even in the comparative cool of England it can reach heights of 27 m and have an umbrage as broad as a beech tree. Its small acorns are food for wood pigeons and squirrels. Sometimes the pigeons eat the acorns clean from the cups, but occasionally they snap the twigs off completely and gather the acorns at leisure from the ground. The squirrels often beat them to it being more agile on the ground while the pigeons crack their wings in a frenzy of manoeuvring, at disadvantage in confined spaces. The *Ilex quercus* reaches its greatest growth along the south coast where it was a popular nineteenth-century introduction, but it is widespread in the region and is found at intervals all along the Old Way, especially in the vicinity of parks.

Wherever there is holly there is almost bound to be ivy. The climbing plant thrives in the damp, shady tangle of old woodland and hedges that bound the Way. Gathering light from the leafless woodland canopy, it has the unusual characteristic of flowering in autumn and producing berries that ripen to a deep purple colour by early spring, giving the birds a much needed source of food when nearly every other berry has gone. The dense evergreen cover is used as winter hibernation by many insects and the fruits are a source of food for winter months. As magic in its properties as holly, ivy was anciently regarded as a safeguard against evil.

The pagan world, linked with holly and ivy, becomes even more palpable as the Way moves east of Wrotham. For the next twenty miles, the countryside is littered with stones, some of them taller than a man. They have smooth, shiny surfaces, deeply pitted even to small holes penetrating right through them. They are made of a hard crystalline sandstone unrelated to local geology and their origin is as conjectural as their name, the sarsens. Sour stones,

Saracen stones – in other words, foreign bodies. Many of them are slumped in the undergrowth, perhaps dragged there by farmers cultivating near-by fields. But many are found by road junctions, some in churchyards and others are erected in such a way that they seem to have special significance, like the White Horse stone at the foot of Bluebell Hill, north of Maidstone.

Any doubts as to their significance in earlier times is dispelled by their use in constructing neolithic tombs, such as the Coldrum Stones a mile east of Trottiscliffe or at Lower Kits Coty, also known as the Countless Stones. The finest construction of the megaliths, the big stones, stands on a hill slope only a quarter of a mile north of the Old Way on the east bank of the river Medway. The three great sarsen slabs supporting a capstone are known to be part of a long barrow, the neolithic tomb of Kits Coty. There are records of landowners blowing up such tombs in the past so other slabs found along the Way may have been so used. Now the Old Way stands revealed for what it really was, a most ancient of ways as old as the tombs, as old as Stonehenge. I wonder what the first pilgrims made of them. Lambarde, writing in the sixteenth century, recorded the local view that Kits Coty was the tomb of the British King Categerne or of the Saxon Horsa who was killed in the battle for the crossing of the Medway.

In this same area are farms bearing names like Cossington and Tottington, the only link with villages that stood there when the first pilgrims passed, but were later visited by the plague and deserted; not the only link, for the grassy banks of old foundations and even the broken walls of a church can be found on the sites. Many of the pilgrims would have sought hospitality at Aylesford Priory, now restored to its old use, or taken a longer diversion to Maidstone. One of their ports of call, still marvellously intact, was the great barn at Boxley, owned by the abbey. What is left of the abbey is now incorporated into a private house, but the stone barn still sprawls its full 57.7 m length in the abbey enclosure. There the abbot gathered his tithes, but the building also housed a medieval brewery and was certainly used as a resting place for pilgrims. One of the products of the present estate is Christmas trees, a nice seasonal touch.

There is a timber barn of a similar size and function at Lenham further east, a survivor of two that stood by the church, symbols of the medieval opulence of the area. Other tithe barns can be found scattered throughout the region, at Sturry in East Kent, at Brook beyond Wye, at Alciston in East Sussex, all standing on what were once ecclesiastical estates. None rival Boxley in its completeness and its incomparable scissor beams supporting the roof. The barn was the pilgrim shelter, but the Miraculous Rood in the church was their objective. The rood has gone, burnt at the Reformation, but the church retains much of interest, not least its unusual entrance by a stone vestibule or narthex fronting the tower. Amongst the tombs are those of the Lushington family, friends and relatives of Lord Tennyson, who was a frequent visitor to the Park House near-by.

From Hollingbourne lies the finest part of the Old Way, a green way winding gently but directly towards its destination. The flora of the bordering shaws is especially rich. The trees and shrubs are worth listing for their sheer variety; field maple, whitebeam, hawthorn, ash, hornbeam, larch, spruce, elder, wayfaring tree, dogwood, hazel, oak, beech, birch, yew, wild plum, wild cherry, Scots pine, holly, spindle, buckthorn, blackthorn, privet, black poplar, wild rose. There are some obvious intruders here, late introductions such as the spruce, the larch and the black poplar, but most of the trees would have been present in the thirteenth century and many would have been familiar to the megalith builders. There is antiquity in the trees as well as the stones.

Tangled up amongst all the trees and shrubs are the white bryony, hanging on with delicate tendrils, and the black bryony twisting round trunks, with its berries every colour from green to scarlet. The roots of the white bryony were cut at one time to sell as a substitute for mandrake, a plant with formidable magic powers. Commonest of the wayside ramblers, lover of lime soils, is Old Man's Beard or Traveller's Joy 'which maketh in winter a goodly shew' according to Gerarde. The long hairy plumes of the *clematis vitalba* give interest to the dullest day. So do the patches of stinking iris opening up their brown pods lined with red berries. Birds peck out the soft vitamin-rich centre of the rose hips and tear the red outer skins back so that they resemble a new flowering. Young oaks hold their brown leaves intact and the field maple, one of the first to yellow, still has leaves on the branches.

On either side are tree plantations and a landscape as trim and well ordered as a parkland, a nice rehearsal for the final miles beyond the palace at Charing where the Old Way runs through three parklands, Eastwell, Godmersham and Chilham. Eastwell, famed in Victorian times for its venison and its greyhounds is mostly under the plough, but within its thirteen-mile perimeter are trees of great age and valleys of quiet charm. Medieval settlements were cleared to make the deer park, the church of Challock being the last reminder of the village that once nestled in a fold of the Downs. By the ruined church at the head of the lake of Eastwell, a gathering place for winter birds, is a large almond tree and, in the churchyard itself, a tomb made of Bethersden marble for Richard, the last of the Plantagenets. Part of the deer park to the north, the King's Wood, has been covered with extensive plantations by the Forestry Commission with several forest walks giving access to new tree-scapes. The evergreens soften the harsher outlines of winter and the carpet of fine needles under the larches (a rare conifer that sheds its leaves seasonally) is kind to the feet after the muddy slopes rising from Boughton Aluph.

The parkland landscapes are survivals of the great sporting estates where the guttural call of the pheasant is as characteristic as the song of the robin. Shooting rights are jealously guarded and the greatest cacophony of sound I have heard in years was by a lodge cottage at Chevening by the breeding enclosure. The small, round eggs are gathered by the bucketful for the winter's sport. The pheasants haunt the hedges and the woodland edge not just for cover but for feeding by scratching away at the ground for their varied diet of acorns, hazel nuts, beechmast, holly berries, hawthorn pips, insects, larvae, snails, slugs, spiders, beetles, woodlice, field mice and voles.

Pheasants were introduced before the Norman conquest as a game bird and are now as much part of the native scene as the wood pigeon or the rook. Partridge suffer much greater variations in number and have been periodically re-introduced to maintain the coveys. They suffer from a loss of their habitat which is typically the rough neglected corners of plough and pasture. The family covey grubbing inconspicuously amongst the turned furrows, speeding to cover with rapid wingbeats is still a fairly common winter sight. The smaller quail, once common, especially on the South Downs, has also suffered from the changes in land use and the loss of its grassland haunts.

Where game birds are reared for shooting, there is still a tendency for other possible and imagined predators to be exterminated. The fences of Eastwell are often lined with the corpses of crows, foxes, moles and magpies, a sight reminiscent of the great northern shoots, where the gamekeeper is king. An unexpected December encounter was with a masked gunman standing silently in the shade of a copse. His quarry were pigeons. The price they fetched on the Continent made the cold wait well worth the effort, a commentary on the rising price of meat and an interesting echo of the large medieval flocks kept by manorial lords for the winter table.

Eastwell was a medieval deer park, but both Godmersham and Chilham were enclosed in later centuries. Godmersham belonged to Jane Austen's brother, Edward Knight who has a memorial in the local church. A plaque of even greater interest for pilgrims is a bas relief of an archbishop taken from a Court Lodge nearby and taken by many to be a representation of Becket himself. At Chilham, the Way diverts from its old course as the seventeenth-century owner emparked the area at the same time as he built a new mansion to replace the Norman castle keep. Appropriately, one of the many rebuilders of the old castle was Henry II, Becket's antagonist. Chilham is a place of more than architectural wonders. Spanish imperial eagles soar over terraces designed by Capability Brown and exotic beasts prowl around the lake he fashioned. The landscape of parklands reveals every change in fashion and Chilham shows all the new devices being used to attract visitors. By the castle gates stands one of the finest village squares in the region with an almost un-broken range of timber-framed buildings, with the church and its massive yew tree tucked away in one corner.

From Chilham it is orchards all the way with occasional patches of woodland, one of them hiding the ramparts of the Iron Age fort of Bigbury. Orchards were the scene of one of the many variants of the wassail at the end of December that was still extant in this century. A cow's horn frightened away the evil spirits, then the finest apple tree was hit with sticks and sprinkled with ale. Stand fast, root, bear well, top. 'Howling' the apples thus was yet another formula for ensuring the next season's bounty. As the track descends from Bigbury to the valley of the Stour, the towers and spires of Canterbury stand in full view and the pilgrims old and new turn their minds to wassails of another kind, feast and festival to celebrate the last days of the year.

Index

INDEX

INDEX

KEY TO ENDPAPER MAPS

NT—National Trust
AM—Ancient Monument

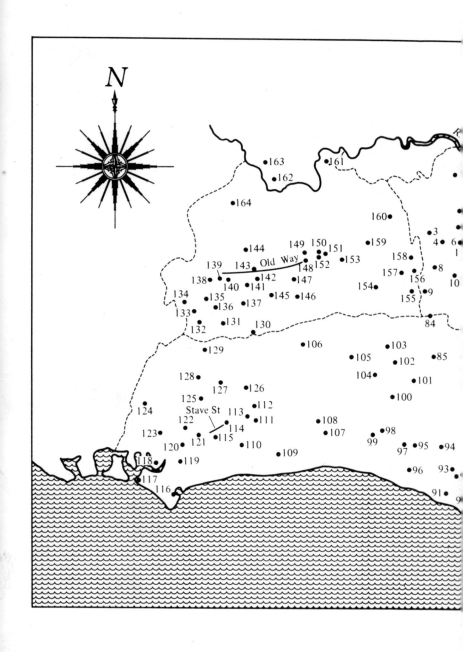